251

Mercantile Bank
is pleased to present to the citizens
of our county

A Pictorial History of Pettis County Missouri
by William B. Claycomb

Proceeds from this beautifully illustrated book
will go to benefit
The Sedalia Area Chamber of Commerce
Katy Depot Project

MERCANTILE
BANK
Member FDIC

PETTIS COUNTY
MISSOURI

A Pictorial History

by

William B. Claycomb

Ed Brummet, *Photograph Editor*

THE
DONNING COMPANY
PUBLISHERS

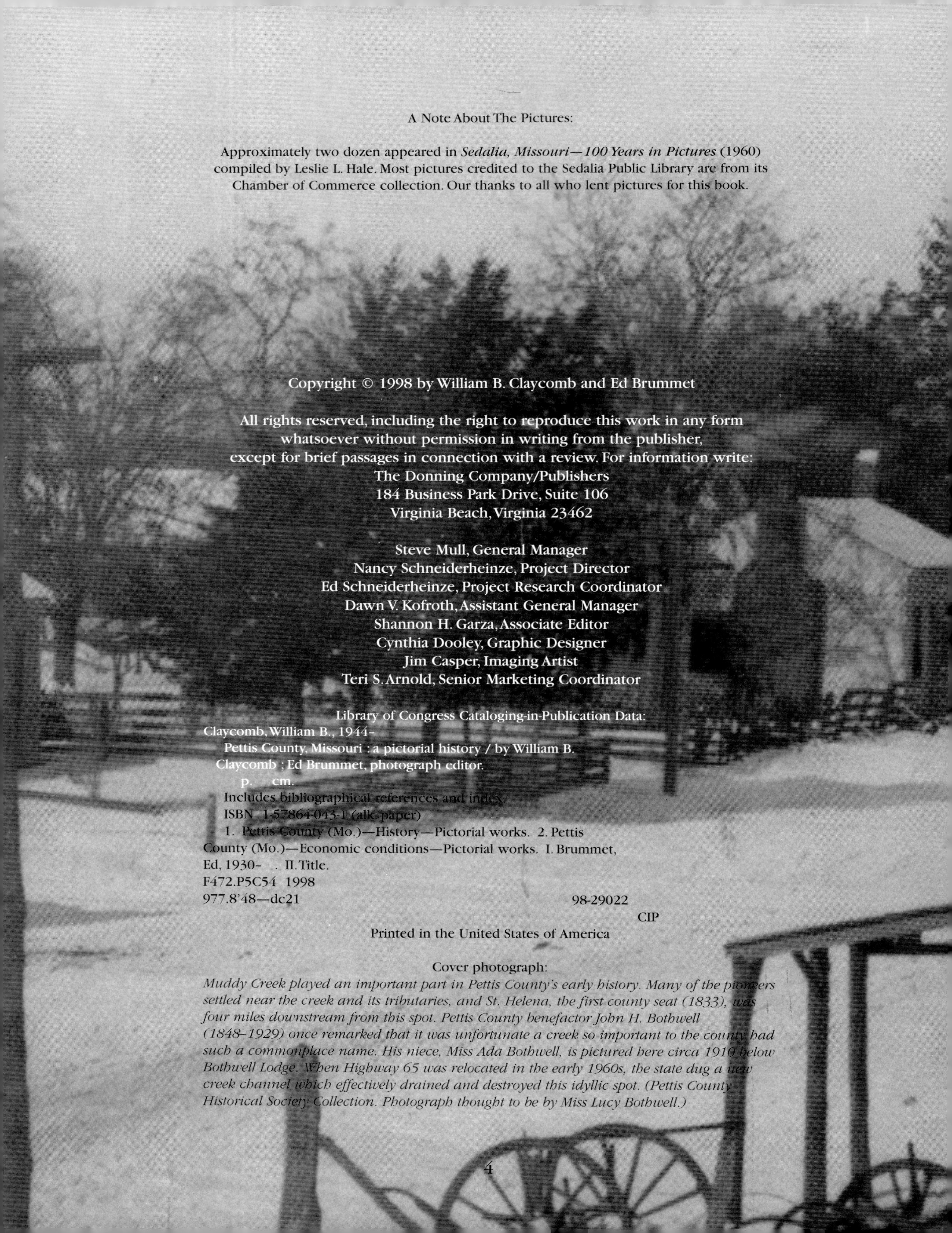

A Note About The Pictures:

Approximately two dozen appeared in *Sedalia, Missouri—100 Years in Pictures* (1960) compiled by Leslie L. Hale. Most pictures credited to the Sedalia Public Library are from its Chamber of Commerce collection. Our thanks to all who lent pictures for this book.

The Donning Company/Publishers
184 Business Park Drive, Suite 106
Virginia Beach, Virginia 23462

Steve Mull, General Manager
Nancy Schneiderheinze, Project Director
Ed Schneiderheinze, Project Research Coordinator
Dawn V. Kofroth, Assistant General Manager
Shannon H. Garza, Associate Editor
Cynthia Dooley, Graphic Designer
Jim Casper, Imaging Artist
Teri S. Arnold, Senior Marketing Coordinator

Library of Congress Cataloging-in-Publication Data:
Claycomb, William B., 1944-
Pettis County, Missouri : a pictorial history / by William B. Claycomb ; Ed Brummet, photograph editor.
p. cm.
Includes bibliographical references and index.
ISBN 1-57864-043-1 (alk. paper)
1. Pettis County (Mo.)—History—Pictorial works. 2. Pettis County (Mo.)—Economic conditions—Pictorial works. I. Brummet, Ed, 1930- . II. Title.
F472.P5C54 1998
977.8'48—dc21 98-29022
CIP

Printed in the United States of America

Cover photograph:
Muddy Creek played an important part in Pettis County's early history. Many of the pioneers settled near the creek and its tributaries, and St. Helena, the first county seat (1833), was four miles downstream from this spot. Pettis County benefactor John H. Bothwell (1848–1929) once remarked that it was unfortunate a creek so important to the county had such a commonplace name. His niece, Miss Ada Bothwell, is pictured here circa 1910 below Bothwell Lodge. When Highway 65 was relocated in the early 1960s, the state dug a new creek channel which effectively drained and destroyed this idyllic spot. (Pettis County Historical Society Collection. Photograph thought to be by Miss Lucy Bothwell.)

Contents

TORE.
TON, BROWN
FOR
GEST IN
WORLD
OE
CO.
AMERICAN FENCE
SOLD
CURITY
CIGARS

Introduction

Pettis County has the distinction of being the place where four of Missouri's geographical areas converge. Each area comprises approximately a quarter of the county which is roughly divided by today's Highways 65 and 50. The northwest quarter is the last of the glacial plains that cover most of north Missouri. The southwest quarter is the beginning of the old Osage prairie that extends southwest into Kansas. The foothills of the Ozarks extend into the county's southeast quarter. And the scenic Boonslick area of bluffs and bottoms extends into the county's northeastern townships. The Missouri General Assembly unintentionally blessed Pettis County with this diverse landscape when it organized it in 1833. Pettis Countians have been enjoying this good fortune since then, if not always aware of it. They have plowed the productive glacial plains and grown corn, wheat, and soybeans. They have bred and fed prize-winning livestock on the limestone soil above the major creeks. They have cleared and farmed those creeks' bottoms. They have built trunk line railroads on the county's high ridges. And at the hub of all this, they have built Sedalia, the self-proclaimed Queen City of the Prairies. Sedalia bestowed this title on itself around the turn of the century when local boosterism was at its height. Yet, the name was not unjustified, especially in the decades after the Civil War when booming Sedalia was the gateway to the Southwest.

While it is landscape that influences a county's history, its men and women make it. Pettis County is a specific piece of land in west central Missouri that you can see on a map, but it is also, and more so, the invisible lives of people who lived (and are living) here. Some Pettis Countians lived here for life; others only passed through. Some brought great distinction to the county; others, notoriety. Whatever their legacies, they contributed to the images of Sedalia and Pettis County we carry in our minds. *Pettis County, Missouri: A Pictorial History*, tells the stories, in words and pictures, of ordinary people within the framework of an extraordinary history.

Chapter One

Above: L. M. Monsees was the country's foremost jack breeder in the years before World War I. His Limestone Valley Farm, shown here on 1909 sale day, was two and one-half miles north of Smithton. Colonel Monsees's residence, right rear, is gone, but the large jack barn in center remains, as does the brick house at left. (Sedalia Public Library Collection)

Left: Detail of the barn

On April 9, 1682, the French explorer Robert LaSalle claimed all the land drained by the Mississippi River for his sovereign, King Louis XIV, and named it Louisiana in the Sun King's honor. The Spanish in Mexico had a vague claim on the territory themselves, but because precious metals had never been found there, they had little interest in it. The French sent some missionaries into the Mississippi Valley to convert the Indians and they founded a few missions and settlements, mainly on the east side of the river.

The French explored the interior of what became Missouri in 1718, and by 1720 Philip Francis Renault, who imported slaves to work for him, was successfully mining for lead in eastern Missouri. The Spanish in Mexico were aware of these French activities and had become concerned about possible French encroachment on their sphere of influence shortly before Renault started his mining operations. Consequently, in 1719 they sent Captain Pedro de Villasur and sixty men on an expedition from Santa Fe to the Missouri River region to determine the extent of French influence in their neglected colony. This expedition met with disaster when Indians massacred all the soldiers except de Villasur himself as told in one story, or a priest in another. Pawnees killed the Spanish on the Platte River in Nebraska, or the Fox and/or Sacs killed them on the Missouri near Malta Bend in Saline County, or, as a third legend has it, the Osage massacred the hapless Spanish in what today is Pettis County.

A ridge rises out of the west Lamine River bottoms one mile north of the mouth of Muddy Creek where the Lamine makes the first of two detours into Pettis County. A hundred feet above the bottom the ridge flattens and at this point one has a panoramic view of the entire river valley, an ideal spot for a camp and/or fortifications in hostile territory. And the spot is less than two miles southeast of the Arrow Rock–Osceola Osage Trail, the Osage's main road from Arrow Rock to their permanent villages on the Osage River in western Missouri. In the Lamine River version of the story, Captain de Villasur invited a group of Missouri Indians to join him in making war on the Osage. In fact, he had mistaken Osage for Missouri Indians. The former returned and in a surprise attack killed all the Spaniards except the hapless captain, who escaped to tell the story. Whether or not the massacre occurred in what became Pettis County 114 years later, remains of fortifications were reported to still be visible in the

1880s and bones were said to have been exhumed from a mound at the site.

Regardless of the true circumstances of the expedition, the French were sufficiently alarmed at the Spaniards' renewed interest in the Missouri River country to establish Fort Orleans in 1722 on the north bank of the Missouri River in extreme southeastern Carroll County, thirty-seven miles directly north of the supposed Lamine River massacre site. The garrison abandoned Fort Orleans five years later.

Renault returned to France in 1742 and, on November 3, 1762, France ceded all its claims to Louisiana to Spain, although it was 1770 before the Spanish took formal control of Upper Louisiana at St. Louis. Having won their independence as well as the Old Northwest from Britain, Americans across the Mississippi River from Spanish Louisiana began to meddle in Spanish affairs, not so much coveting the territory as wanting a guarantee of free passage down the Mississippi to the port of New Orleans. And because Upper Louisiana was underpopulated, the Spanish authorities in St. Louis invited American settlers into their territory. Men like Daniel Boone accepted the invitation. The aggressive Americans had a foothold west of the Mississippi.

Having become a pawn in European politics, Spain once again ceded Louisiana to France on October 1, 1800. First Consul, soon-to-be-Emperor, Napoleon decided to sell it to the United States in 1803, realizing the territory would make the United States more powerful and therefore a more potent counterbalance to Britain in North America. He also needed the money. Napoleon is reported to have felt that should he ever want Louisiana, or at least New Orleans, back, he could easily enough take it. The formal transfer of power occurred at St. Louis on March 9–10, 1804. At four cents per acre, cash and claims, Pettis County's 686 square miles cost the United States $17,561.60.

The new government had at least two problems: sorting out and recognizing the old French and Spanish land grants, and moving the Indians west of the frontier. In what became Pettis County, land titles were not a problem because neither the French nor Spanish had granted any. As for the Indians, the Osage presence took care of itself when the Osages (who had never had permanent villages in Pettis County) asked the United States for protection from their enemies. The United States saw an opportunity, and the Treaty of Fort Osage, agreed upon November 10, 1808, effectively moved the Osage out of Missouri except what became the western tier of counties. This opened west central Missouri to settlement. The War of 1812 stopped the first tentative visits to the county by potential squatters and settlers. But with the British and their Indian allies more or less defeated, the first permanent white settlers entered what became northeast Pettis County in 1817.

Until the frontier was surveyed, everyone was, by definition, a squatter, unless they had title to old French and/or Spanish land grants. It is not known when the land of Pettis County was surveyed and subdivided into congressional townships of thirty-six square miles each, each of the thirty-six "section" corners marked with rocks, but it was probably done by 1823. The surveyor's work goes unnoticed in the history books, but there would have been no orderly settlement of the West without his backbreaking and remarkably accurate work, considering his simple tools. At any rate, the pioneers of Pettis were squatters for at least six years. They had chosen what seemed to them to be favorable sites south of Heath's Creek along its tributaries. The early homesteads were always near wood and water. While the woods provided game, logs, and fuel, the streams supplied fish and drinking water, although springs probably provided most of the latter.

The pioneers had several things in common—poverty, lack of law, and abundant courage, among others. There was very little "hard currency" in Pettis County in the early years. Commerce and debt were transacted on pieces of paper—IOU's passed between and among the pioneers in lieu of money—for years, in some cases, before finally being paid. After Thomas Wasson established his gristmill on Muddy Creek at Pin Hook, a village grew up around the mill that attracted two merchants—Sappington and Marmaduke, and the Wood Brothers, Clifton and Watson. These merchants acted as bankers for the community. The Sappington and Marmaduke Store closed when Georgetown became the county seat in 1837. But the Wood Brothers remained in the county and prospered, first in Georgetown and later in Sedalia, becoming wealthy not only from their mercantile business, but also from their role as unofficial bankers until 1866, when the county's first bank, the First National Bank of Sedalia, was chartered.

Until 1833, the nearest civil law for those living in what became the eastern tier of townships, then part of Cooper County, was at Boonville.

The rest of Pettis County was attached to Saline County, with the county seat variously located at Old Jefferson, Jonesboro (Napton), and Arrow Rock. There was little law, but with a small and scattered population, and no lawyers, there was little need for it.

In 1828 a voting precinct was established two miles southwest of Longwood at the home of Jesse Swope. Longwood, founded circa 1819 on a hill south of Heath's Creek, was first called Hermantown. It was a stage stop on the Boonville-Independence Road as well as the Miami-Warsaw Road. Before the Civil War, Longwood residents moved their village a quarter mile south to its present location. A single brick house remains at the original site.

It is estimated there were some seven hundred people living in what was about to become Pettis County by 1833. On January 28 of that year the General Assembly took the western side of Cooper and the south two-thirds of Saline, created a new county, and called it Pettis in honor of the late and lamented Congressman Spencer Pettis, a protégé of Senator Thomas Hart Benton killed in a foolhardy duel by Major Thomas Biddle, who died at St. Louis in 1831. St. Helena, known variously as Pin Hook or Ramey and Wasson's Mill, was designated the temporary seat of justice. It is unclear where court was actually held—the mill itself, a shed, or, more likely, Judge James Ramey's house. In 1835 Pettis lost most of its south half to Benton County, but regained twenty-four square miles on the southwest in 1845.

By this time of organization there was a German settlement in southeast Pettis County and a settlement of Carolinians at Buncombe in the east central part to supplement the mostly Kentucky pioneers scattered along Muddy, Flat, and Heath's Creeks. The western townships were sparsely settled. All of the original county officers were appointed by the governor, and the first term of circuit court was held at St. Helena July 8, 1833, with Judge John Ferguson Ryland presiding. From this rustic start on the isolated west central Missouri prairie, in less than fifty years, Pettis County ranked ninth in population among the state's 114 counties, and was one of the most prosperous.

Chapter Two

Left: Thomas Wasson built his gristmill here on Muddy Creek eight miles northeast of Sedalia in the 1820s. St. Helena, also known as Pin Hook, the county's first seat of justice, was located to the left. The hamlet vanished after the county seat was moved to Georgetown in 1837. (William B. Claycomb Collection)

Above: Detail of Muddy Creek

The pace of migration into Pettis County picked up almost immediately after its organization. The most prominent immigrant in 1833 was General David Thomson of Georgetown, Kentucky. General Thomson, a distinguished and well-to-do Kentuckian at the age of fifty-eight, decided there was opportunity in west central Missouri for himself and his family, which in this case numbered about ninety including seventy-five slaves. The slaves were his own and those of his sons-in-law, Lewis Redd Major and George R. Smith. He had previously purchased six hundred acres at $1.25 per acre two miles northwest of what was soon to become Georgetown. In 1840 he built a no-frills but handsome federal brick house on his farm and named it Elm Spring. Lewis Major built a similar but more impressive house a mile north on his farm. Both houses remain—Elm Spring, in good shape; the Major house, long abandoned. George Smith's first house on Muddy Creek was burned, reportedly by one of his slaves. General Thomson also built a gristmill on Muddy Creek near his home and otherwise improved his farm.

Thomson differed from the earlier Pettis pioneers, including the worthy Reuben Estes Gentry and his promising sons who lived four miles east at Wood Dale Farm, because of the financial resources he was able to bring with him. The second generation of Gentrys would eclipse the Thomsons with the possible exception of the notoriously opinionated George R. Smith, founder of Sedalia. But during his lifetime in Pettis County, General Thomson was highly respected as a patriarch. When the new county seat town was being surveyed, officials gave him the honor of naming it. He named it after his Kentucky hometown.

General Thomson and his sons-in-law paid the going rate for their farms, the maximum price the government asked. While $1.25 an acre was a deliberately modest price (the government wanted to make land available to as many settlers as possible), the U.S. Treasury made a comfortable profit, considering it paid the French about four cents an acre for it. However, taking into account the cost of moving the Indians off it and the additional cost of surveying and selling it, the profit margin shrinks somewhat.

In part because of the government's liberal land policy which encouraged immigration, the county's population is estimated to have quadrupled between 1833 and 1840. The population in 1840 was:

Free White Males	1,236
Free White Females	1,141
	2,377
Free Black Male	1
Male Slaves	264
Female Slaves	288
	552
Total	2,930

St. Helena was located in this field just east of Muddy Creek on the old Osage, later Arrow Rock–Osceola Trail. Its two stores and gristmill served a wide area between Arrow Rock and Warsaw in the frontier days. The clump of trees on right is reportedly the site of the community's well. (William B. Claycomb Collection)

There was only one free black man among the population of nearly three thousand. Slaves made up some 19 percent of the 1840 population. Their numbers more than tripled by 1860, but their percentage of total population increased only slightly to twenty percent on the eve of the Civil War.

County officials moved to the new two-story brick courthouse in Georgetown in the fall of 1837. The contractors were George R. Smith and Judge James Ramey and its cost was $4,000. There was enough money to add a decorative cupola topped with a spire, gold globe, and an arrow-fish weathervane, according to Smith's daughter Martha E. Smith. The cupola and its spire had little if any practical use, but they could be construed as an early indication of the county's nascent wealth. It is regrettable that Judge Ramey, a man who played an important role in the early years of the county, lies in a now unmarked grave on *Oakdale*, Major William Gentry's place southwest of Georgetown.

George Heard, the first lawyer to make a permanent settlement in Pettis County, arrived at St. Helena in 1835 at age twenty-six. He soon built the first house in Georgetown where he taught the first school in the county. By practicing two professions that symbolized "progress," he represented the county's growing "civilization." The father of two sons, both attorneys—Congressman John T. Heard and George C. Heard—George Heard lived on his 340-acre farm a quarter mile east of Crown Hill Cemetery in his later years.

Milton Thomson, son of General David Thomson and a graduate of West Point, was the county's second teacher. The early schools were private, but on November 7, 1853, the county court appointed Aldea A. Glasscock, a lawyer who lived on a farm in extreme northeastern Pettis County, the first county school commissioner. It was not until after the Civil War that school districts were fully organized.

Besides the growing interest in education, there was an even earlier interest in religion. Churches were established among the settlements at this time, with the first probably being what is now known as Mount Herman north of Sedalia on the old Georgetown–Arrow Rock Road. The early churches, all Protestant, were organized by clergymen who often moved on once a church was chartered and operating.

Most of the early attorneys have been forgotten, but the generation that arrived in the decade before the Civil War produced at least two U.S. Congressmen, one U.S. Senator, and several circuit judges, starting a tradition of a distinguished Pettis County Bar that continued into the twentieth century.

Doctors, too, were available in the early days, although some seem not to have had formal training and practiced medicine as a sideline to other pursuits. For example, Dr. Moses A. Ferris settled one mile south of Longwood about 1833. Not only did he practice medicine, he also was a "Reformed" preacher and a livestock breeder, reportedly importing the first purebred cattle into the county. He served as a surgeon for a company of Kentucky volunteers in the War of 1812. On the other hand, after the Civil War Sedalia attracted highly educated physicians with impressive experience. For instance, Dr. Thomas B. Memminger studied medicine in Charleston, New York, and Paris, served as a high-ranking surgeon in the Confederate Army throughout the war, and entered private practice afterward, eventually coming to Sedalia in 1881. He was the son of Christopher G. Memminger of South Carolina, secretary of the treasury of the Confederate States of America (a thankless job).

The point is, even before the county seat was moved from St. Helena to Georgetown, there was already a small class of professionals trying to earn livings in a primitive place that was not far east of the frontier.

Georgetown by the 1850s was one of the major towns of west central Missouri. It was the scene of a good deal of trade—local and to the southwest—and boasted a population of about fifteen hundred. The rise of Sedalia doomed it by 1865.

Although the 1840s were a time of growth for the county, it remained relatively isolated because it did not border a major river. The roads were little better than the old Indian trails, and Eastern markets remained out of reach of Pettis County farmers, although there was little surplus to sell. Ironically, given that the county's own transportation system was so poor, Pettis County in the 1840s was home to some of the West's greatest transportation pioneers. These freighters did an immense business on the Plains before the Civil War.

James Brown (1801–1850) arrived in Georgetown in 1837. He soon bought 1,200 acres two miles east of town and commenced freighting on the Plains, doing business as Brown and Company. In 1848 he received the first army contract to supply the garrison at Santa Fe. He was successful and paved the way for future freighters to operate on the Great Plains under contract to the U.S. Army. The risks were great, including ambush by hostile Indians and deadly weather (Brown himself got caught in a blizzard outside Santa Fe and died there), but the rewards were also great if freight was delivered as agreed.

The most distinguished freighter was John S. Jones (1811–1876) of Longwood, who came to Pettis County from Natchez, Mississippi, in 1845. Prior to his emigration to Missouri, Jones managed a plantation for Jefferson Davis and married a cousin of the future president of the Confederacy. Jones improved a showplace 2,200-acre farm southwest of Longwood he called *Deer Park* after the Davis plantation at Natchez. He was freighting on the Great Plains by 1849, bidding for the lucrative army and postal contracts and working in partnership with a succession of men, including James Brown, William H. Russell of Lexington, Dr. Joseph L. Cartwright of Longwood, and others. His younger brother, Charles, was his assistant for many years. The firm of Jones and Cartwright was the first freighter into Denver. In 1859 Jones and Russell founded the Leavenworth and Pike's Peak Express Company, the first overland stage line to Denver, and later that year they organized the Central Overland California and Pike's Peak Express Company, better known as the Pony Express, with Jones serving as superintendent. This company was capitalized at $200,000, an enormous amount at the time. The failure of the Pony Express forced Jones into bankruptcy and he and his family abandoned *Deer Park* for Colorado shortly after the Civil War began. For the last fifteen years of his life he engaged in business, built mountain roads and a railroad, helped charter the University of Colorado at Boulder, and otherwise prepared the territory for statehood.

Besides Brown, Jones, and Cartwright, there were other Pettis Countians on the western trails, such as Reuben Gentry, Jr., who successfully freighted into Mexico City just prior to the Mexican War. They have all been unfairly neglected by historians, but two of them, Brown and Jones, rank high among the important freighters.

By 1850 the county's population had increased 76 percent from the 1840 census to a total of 5,150: 4,261 whites, 884 slaves, and 5 free blacks. The county's population and wealth continued to grow in the 1850s, in part due to the influx of a group of affluent Kentuckians from the Blue Grass region. Most of these men bought vast tracts on the prairie in what would become the Hughesville neighborhood. They improved their farms with splendid frame houses and set their slaves and sons to breaking the sod and cultivating crops. As these estates were near Heath's Creek, the old Georgetown settlers referred to the newly arrived Kentuckians as the "Heath's Creek aristocrats." The professional men among them, such as lawyers George G. Vest and John F. Philips, lived in Georgetown. Most of these families were members of the First Church of Pettis (Old School Presbyterian Church), established in 1856. In 1859, under the capable leadership of the Reverend Dr. John Montgomery, they built a forty-by-sixty-foot brick church on the site of today's High Point Cemetery.

The county's increasing wealth is reflected in the price of land. The Kentuckians who came in 1853 paid as little as $5 an acre for some of their land. Those who bought their farms in 1860 paid Eastern speculators and locals up to $20 an acre.

Arguably the oldest extant building in Pettis County, these ruins are located one-half mile north of Longwood. The house was built in the early 1840s as a combination stagecoach stop and residence, and is now owned by Jean Callis Edwards. (William B. Claycomb Collection)

If these men thought they would be safe in west central Missouri, an area that reminded them of home, in the upcoming sectional conflict, they were disappointed. When the Civil War came, they found not only their property in danger, but their lives as well.

Loyalties were fairly evenly divided among Northern Unionists, Southern rebels, and those who professed neutrality, but the Southern sympathizers, who were not confined to the "Heath's Creek aristocrats," suffered most, in part because Pettis County would remain in Union hands (except for one afternoon) throughout the war, and there was no one to protect them from Union depredations.

As the 1850s drew to a close, two things were about to change the county forever—the Pacific Railroad and the Civil War. The old agrarian society based on a fairly self-sufficient economy was not going to vanish, but as the county was linked to Eastern and later Southwestern markets by the railroads, that society was going to change, resulting in the loss of influence of the old order and opportunity for others.

The railroad came to Missouri for local, sectional, and national reasons: to carry produce to market and encourage industrial development; the desire of Missouri and the South to develop territory open to slavery at least as fast as that made free by the Missouri Compromise; and the need to bind the East to the newly acquired West by a transcontinental railroad.

The railroad came to Sedalia for one reason: the efforts of George R. Smith (1804–1879). The railroad engineers and a majority of citizens favored the Missouri River route west of Jefferson City through prosperous and populous river counties. But a minority of citizens and politicians, led by Smith, promoted the more direct inland route across the relatively sparsely settled Pettis and Johnson Counties. In the end, the issue boiled down to who could offer the railroad more money. In August 1852, Pettis County voted to subscribe to $100,000 in railroad stock. The six other inland counties also voted several hundred thousands in stock. On December 25, 1852, the General Assembly passed legislation locating the railroad along the inland route contingent upon the seven counties raising another $400,000 in one year. Pettis County's quota was $70,000. Largely due to Smith's vigorous efforts, $412,000 was subscribed and on November 14, 1853, the board of directors of the Pacific Railroad voted to locate the railroad on the inland route.

Resigned that the engineers would not be persuaded to survey the route into Georgetown, Smith purchased 503 acres on the survey three miles south of Georgetown from Absalom McVey for $6,521, or $13 an acre. The first lots were sold in October 1860, and three months later, on January 17, 1861, the first passenger train arrived in Sedalia. The road's progress west to Kansas City was stopped by the Civil War for two years, and Sedalia became a Union Army garrison and headquarters town.

George R. Smith was a difficult man. He was an outspoken and tactless ingrate who quarreled with business partners and political enemies and allies alike. Yet he had two redeeming qualities: his vision of Sedalia and his devotion to his two daughters, who seem to have worshipped him.

Smith received his title of general when he was commissioned brigadier general of state militia in 1838 during the so-called Mormon War. He served one month, reportedly never left Georgetown, and saw no action. On August 24, 1861, Governor Hamilton Gamble named him adjutant general of Missouri. He soon quarreled with Gamble and resigned three months later. In 1843 President Polk had appointed him receiver of public moneys at Springfield, Missouri. Polk removed him a year later when Smith openly criticized the administration. During the Civil War he called General U. S. Grant "that little imbecile" because of his support of President Lincoln's policy of reconciliation. In 1865 President Andrew Johnson named Smith assessor of internal revenue, and on schedule Smith denounced Johnson as a traitor. He lost that job ten months after being named to it. He ran for Pettis County representative five times and was defeated four. He ran for Congress three times and withdrew once and was defeated twice. He *was* elected to the State Senate in 1864, but resigned the next year to take the assessor job. He was also elected charter mayor of Sedalia in 1864 and served three months. Finally in 1874 he was elected an alderman of Sedalia.

Smith was a Whig before the war, but converted to Radical Republicanism in 1862. A co-author of the notoriously vindictive Drake Constitution that punished Missouri Southern sympathizers by disfranchising them, he was one of the state's most vociferous Radicals, despised by many. But despite his many faults, it was his hard work and determination that brought the railroad to the county, and Sedalia to the railroad. He died in his mansion on East Broadway and left a fortune to his daughters, who, to their credit, gave part of it to Sedalia in the form of real estate for a college for blacks, a park, and a high school, among other benefactions. In 1866 Smith himself sold the courthouse block to the county for $5.

The county's population on the eve of the Civil War was 9,392: 7,506 whites, 1,880 slaves, and 6 free blacks. This was an 82 percent increase for the decade.

When war finally came, both sides actively recruited in Pettis County.

Oakdale, *residence of Major William Gentry three miles northwest of Sedalia, was one of the finest of Pettis County's antebellum houses. Built by Gentry in 1852, it remained in his family (except for about twenty-five years early in the twentieth century) until 1995 when Mr. and Mrs. Charles Curry bought it. (William B. Claycomb Collection)*

Georgetown lawyer John F. Philips was commissioned colonel of the Seventh Cavalry, Missouri State Militia, and he recruited 623 of his 978 men from Pettis County. The remainder came from Johnson and Saline Counties. This regiment saw a good deal of bloody action for three years in Missouri, none of it at home. The ranks of the Fortieth Regiment Enrolled Missouri Militia, Colonel R. R. Spedden commanding, were largely filled with Pettis Countians. In addition, there was a home guard unit that did some service in the area.

Colonel Ebenezer Magoffin, one of the most prominent "Heath's Creek aristocrats," was a successful Confederate recruiter until his capture by Union forces in Johnson County in December 1861. He quartered his recruits at Prairie Lea, his 2,160-acre estate in Hughesville Township, until sending them south to join General Sterling Price. (Colonel Magoffin killed the first Union soldier in Pettis County in a skirmish in Georgetown on August 29, 1861.)

Colonels Philips, Spedden, Magoffin, and their staff officers were educated gentlemen, if amateur soldiers. Not all soldiers stationed in the county were gentlemen; some posing as soldiers were in fact criminals using the confusion of war as cover for their crimes. These latter, out-of-control irregulars and bushwhackers, were rightfully feared by law-abiding citizens as well as regular soldiers. But while they committed random atrocities, the most outrageous atrocities were committed by uniformed troops. For instance, on October 15, 1864, 1,500 Confederate cavalry under General Jeff Thompson, part of Price's army, captured Sedalia, lightly defended by 250 to 300 Home Guards. General Thompson's orderly sergeant, Sergeant Helm, was shot dead in the back while under a flag of truce by Frank McCabe of the Home Guards. A second Confederate trooper was shot and killed nearby as he tried to res-

William H. Field built "Eldon" in 1854 on his 1,700-acre farm four miles southwest of Longwood. Field, 54, was taken from this house on June 5, 1862, by Union troops under the command of Lieutenant George Nash, falsely accused of receiving stolen Union property and harboring Confederate marauders, and shot. His death shocked the state and Nash was eventually tried for murder in Jefferson City. He vanished before the verdict. The house burned in 1880. (Karen Chamberlin Collection)

cue a comrade pinned beneath his horse. This shameful conduct paled, however, beside the Confederate mass execution of ten blacks who had helped the Home Guard dig trenches. For good measure, they also burned homes in the black neighborhood. Meanwhile, the Confederates looted at will until General Thompson arrived from Georgetown where he had been visiting friends. He got his cavalry under control and rejoined Price, lumbering toward his Westport showdown with the Union Army.

Regular Union officers also killed civilians in cold blood, and their men were not above robbing the locals. On June 5, 1862, Lieutenant George Nash unjustly ordered the murder of William H. Field, a wealthy lawyer and landowner who lived four miles southwest of Longwood, on suspicion of receiving stolen Federal supplies. Union troops helped themselves to Colonel Magoffin's property even when it was under the temporary protection of headquarters. These are only two examples out of dozens perpetrated in Pettis County during the war. Other counties suffered more, especially the border counties south of Kansas City. There was never a major battle in Pettis County. With Union garrisons at Sedalia, the railroad terminus, and the crossroads towns of Georgetown, Longwood, and Dunksburg, local conflicts were limited to skirmishes and light casualties. Nevertheless, when the war was done, families were displaced and Pettis County's sons lay in hundreds of graves scattered far from home. And those returning home, Union and Confederate alike, found new leadership, new money, and unfamiliar faces installed in the new county seat town of Sedalia.

Chapter Three

Left: Pettis Countians gather in the woods for a rustic dance and picnic in the 1890s. The location may be Bowling Green Township. (Pettis County Historical Society Collection)

Above: Detail of the gathering

This is the earliest known picture of Sedalia and dates from circa 1868. It looks west down Main Street from Lamine Street. Fred's Restaurant and Mackey's Boots and Shoes are visible on the right, on north side of Main. Laid out parallel to the Pacific Railroad tracks, all of Sedalia between Clay and Third Streets angles slightly toward the northwest. (Ed Brummet Collection)

In 1866 Pettis County was firmly under the control of Radical Republicans, all appointed by the Radical administration in Jefferson City. Armed with the Drake Constitution, the Radicals were interested in doing their own reconstruction in Missouri. One of their most effective tools was the so-called Test Oath, administered by a new official, registrar of voters. All former Southern sympathizers were disfranchised, and professionals could not practice unless they swore allegiance before the registrar of voters. In Pettis County the registrar was the zealous Major Bacon Montgomery, a young man who published the first newspaper in the county just prior to the war, then joined the Union Army and built a distinguished record as a cavalry officer in the lower Mississippi Valley. After the war he was commissioned first colonel and finally brigadier general of state militia as reward for his heavy-handed "pacification" of unreconstructed Lafayette County in 1866. If one wanted to preach, teach, practice medicine or law, or just vote, he took the hated oath before General Montgomery. The U.S. Supreme Court eventually found the oath unconstitutional and the Radical Republicans lost control of the state and county first to the Liberal Republicans and then in 1872 to the Democrats, who retained control for a generation.

The county court, led by Judge E. W. Washburn, was busy. Besides moving the roads off the old trails to the surveyed section lines, the court aggressively built railroads. It turned its attention first to the old Tebo and

Neosho Railroad, which had been chartered March 20, 1860. Newly arrived Sedalia bankers Cyrus Newkirk and Colonel A. D. Jaynes secured the old charter about 1866, and Sedalia subscribed $50,000 in stock to build southwest to Fort Scott, Kansas. Pettis County subscribed to first $75,000 and later $200,000 in stock to build northeast to Boonville. Groundbreaking for the southwest extension of what was now the Missouri-Kansas and Texas Railroad was held September 18, 1867, and the first train to Clinton ran July 23, 1870. By November 1873, the line was open between Hannibal, Missouri, and Denison, Texas. Meanwhile, in 1870 the MK&T established shops between Fifth Street and Broadway east of the tracks. In 1873 the railroad's general offices were built on the northeast corner of Broadway and Hancock, east of the new shops. This large two-story brick building served as the general headquarters until 1881 when the road became part of the Gould system.

The county court next turned its attention to an old 1858 charter granted by the state to build a railroad between Lexington and Farmers' City on the Pacific Railroad three miles east of what was to become Sedalia. By 1867 Sedalia was fixed as the intersection point and Pettis County issued $110,000 in construction bonds. Work commenced on the fifty-five-mile railroad April 11, 1869, and it opened for business in 1871 with two trains each way per day. This road, officially the Lexington and St. Louis Railroad, was operated by and later sold to the Missouri Pacific and was known as the Lexington Branch of that railroad.

In 1879 Cyrus Newkirk and other Sedalians induced Benton County to give Sedalia the unfinished roadbed of the Osage Valley and Southern Kansas Railroad Company which had been projected to run from Warsaw to connect with the Missouri Pacific at Tipton. Since Pettis County was at

J. R. Barrett, prominent Sedalia businessman who owned seven hundred acres west of Grand Avenue, built the Barrett Hotel in the early 1870s at the southwest corner of South Grand and Clinton Road on the MK&T mainline. Besides a hotel, it served as the Katy's headquarters and general hospital for a short time before becoming the Sedalia University in 1882. It burned several years later. (Ed Brummet Collection)

Absalom McVey was survived by his third wife, Lucinda Allison. Each of McVey's three wives bore him eight children. His donation of land to the Pacific Railroad assured Sedalia's and General George R. Smith's future. (Ed Brummet Collection)

J. West Goodwin started publishing the Bazoo *on September 20, 1869. The flamboyant Goodwin published his newspaper for decades. Philip Werner's liquor and grocery store was on the ground floor at 211 South Ohio. (Sedalia Public Library Collection)*

Above, left: The old Broadway School was built in 1867 and opened for business February 10, 1868. Although not the first school in Sedalia, it was the first public school. It is now the site of Third National Bank. (Ed Brummet Collection)

Above, right: The Looney and Bloess Lumber Company was originally on West Pacific Street. Joe Woods was lynched in 1867 in the arch at right. (Ed Brummet Collection)

its debt limit by now, $40,000 was raised privately by Newkirk and his partners and in November 1879, work started between Sedalia and Cole Camp on a narrow-gauge railroad, now named the Sedalia, Warsaw, and Southwestern Railroad. Freight and passenger service started the summer of 1881. The three-feet narrow gauge was later converted to the standard gauge of four feet and eight and one-half inches when the Missouri Pacific gained control of the road. This branch line was abandoned and dismantled in 1946.

Judge Washburn's Radical court floated several hundred-thousand-dollar bond issues in secret to construct railroads without consulting public opinion. And although the court had the legal right at the time to issue bonds without public approval, political opponents demanded the recall of the Pettis County Court, and even its abolition. Some taxpayers refused to pay the railroad tax and the railroads eventually had to sue the county in federal court to pay the bonds. In the Radicals' defense, however, by 1883 there were 928 employees of all railroads in town, 110 locomotives were reportedly stationed in Sedalia, and the town had become a minor Midwestern railroad hub. Sedalia as well as Hughesville, Houstonia, Green Ridge, and even Valda south of Sedalia now had direct access to the great cities and their markets. The county's debt was eventually paid and citizens came to take the railroads for granted.

It was those railroads, as well as mechanization, that changed farm life in the postwar years. The mechanization of agriculture increased grain production, and the railroads transported the county's surplus grain and livestock to theretofore inaccessible markets. The 1870 agricultural statistics

Sedalia citizens organized a Fire and Hook and Ladder Company in February 1867. On November 6, 1867, fire destroyed many buildings in the 100 block of West Main Street, doing some $90,000 in damage. (Ed Brummet Collection)

for Pettis County reported 196,024 acres, or about 44 percent of the county, were under cultivation; 79,282 acres were woodland; and the balance, 38 percent, was "unimproved." The cash value of the county's farms was $7,475,690; machinery and equipment were $248,612; and wages were $154,817. Farm products were valued at $1,535,401 and livestock was $1,595,244. The county produced everything from 9,958 pounds of tobacco to 11,159 pounds of honey, including 385 gallons of wine.

The prosperity of the postwar years was cut short by the Panic of 1873. The supply of farm products by then exceeded the demand, prices fell drastically, and loans that could not be paid came due at banks. Looking for someone to blame, the farmers, among others, blamed the railroads, who were perceived to be riding roughshod over their customers, especially their smaller ones, by charging them whatever the traffic would bear. The perception was in fact the case, as the unregulated railroads were indeed charging freight rates worthy of monopolies, although favoring some of their biggest customers with sweetheart deals. Farmers and their allies felt betrayed because their taxes had largely built the railroads. Some farmers organized Granges and supported the People's Party's candidate for governor in 1874, Major William Gentry of Pettis County, who ran on a platform that included some regulation of railroads (although he had himself been president of two—the Lexington Branch and the Warsaw Road). Gentry was defeated, but the victorious Democrats did impose some regulation on the railroads and instituted other reforms. Better times returned to Pettis County's farms. The county is ideally suited for livestock production because of its grain production, proximity to Ozark "feeders," and almost perfect conditions for livestock—grass, water, and plenty of natural shelter. The county's most distinguished livestock feeders and breeders started their careers in this last quarter of the nineteenth century.

Meanwhile, fortunes were being made in Sedalia, mostly by Union veterans who came to Sedalia at the close of the war. Conspicuous among this group of entrepreneurs were Colonel A. D. Jaynes, Cyrus Newkirk, and David H. Smith of Ohio, Orestes Crandall of Illinois, and, somewhat younger, John H. Bothwell also of Illinois. Jaynes and Newkirk were bankers and railroad promoters; Smith was a hardware merchant; Crandall was a financier; and Bothwell was a lawyer, politician, and businessman. The fortunes of the old families were predicated on real estate. George R. Smith developed all of downtown and central Sedalia; J. R. Barrett's farm west of Grand Avenue became west Sedalia; and Absalom McVey's farm

Late nineteenth century Sedalia firemen show off their equipment in front of the longtime fire station at 211 South Kentucky. The old building was finally replaced and demolished in the 1960s. (Ed Brummet Collection)

Farriers performed important services in the days before automobiles. This gentleman with a watch fob combined horseshoeing with wagon and carriage repair. (Ed Brummet Collection)

(what he did not sell to Smith) was subdivided into east Sedalia. Major William Gentry's wealth was based on almost 6,000 acres of prime Pettis County land. He actually lived three miles northwest of town, but was closely associated with its banking and railroad interests, as well as engaged in extensive farming operations.

While the railroads expanded their presence in Sedalia and businessmen were outdoing each other building ornate brick and stone buildings downtown, vice was also booming, if not quite so obviously, along both sides of the Missouri Pacific tracks. Sedalia's reputation for prostitution and corruption dates from the postwar decades, and that reputation lingered through World War II. Also, while Colonel Jaynes, Mr. Newkirk, D. H. Smith, George R. Smith, and the others were building magnificent mansions on Broadway, thousands of laborers were living in modest frame houses and shacks in east Sedalia, and the emerging middle class families were buying or building increasingly comfortable houses west of Ohio Street. Somewhere between these classes were hundreds of men, mostly bachelors, who lived in boarding houses across town. Many of these men worked for the railroads, but dozens were professionals who lived at the Garrison House (site of present Missouri Pacific Depot) and other upscale establishments.

In 1881 Jay Gould, who already controlled the Missouri Pacific, gained control of the Katy Railroad and made it a division of the Missouri Pacific, called the Kansas and Texas Division of the Missouri Pacific. The Katy's general headquarters building at East Broadway and Hancock was converted to a hospital for the Missouri Pacific, reportedly the third railroad hospital in the country. In 1882 the Katy Hospital moved from the old Barrett Hotel at the southwest corner of Grand Avenue and Clinton Road to Broadway and Hancock, and the two operations were combined in a single hospital. Dr. Willis P. King was chief surgeon. In 1889 the Missouri Pacific Hospital was transferred to Kansas City, but the Katy Hospital with 125 beds remained in Sedalia under the direction of chief surgeon Dr. E. F. Yancey, a post he held for over forty years beginning January 1, 1891. He supervised two physicians, one druggist, eight Sisters of Charity nurses, and a dozen orderlies, as well as over one hundred local surgeons throughout the 2,500-mile Katy system. He was also the Missouri Pacific's local surgeon in the 1890s. The hospital, which received an average one dozen admissions a day, was supported by an assessment from all Katy employees in ratio to their wages.

Railroad work was dangerous and the Katy Hospital was busy. The Interstate Commerce Commission reported May 5, 1903, that, in 1902, 190 railroad employees were killed and 23,023 injured nationwide while coupling and uncoupling cars, despite newly enacted "automatic coupler laws." The Sedalia newspapers reported accidents at the local shops almost daily, often involving the feet. Engineers and conductors were also frequently injured or killed on the road.

The Katy Hospital closed circa 1938; it was demolished and the block leased to the city for a park until sold and commercially developed in the 1960s.

Above, left: This may be the interior of the Ilmberger and Son wagonworks. A new wagon bed awaits its wheels. (Ed Brummet Collection)

Above, right: Ernest Lamy's first brick building was destroyed in the 1867 fire. Most of this building was constructed the next year and remains in use as a work clothing factory. J. A. Lamy, Ernest's son, sold the company to the Stafford family in 1912. This picture dates from the early 1960s. (Sedalia Public Library Collection)

Sedalia fire wagons doubled as parade floats in the 1890s. The little girl is almost lost among the flowers. (Ed Brummet Collection)

Both railroads operated stockyards in Sedalia from the earliest days into the 1950s. In 1865 the Missouri Pacific located a stockyard on five acres near East Broadway and Marshall. Chiefly for local use, it could handle fifteen hundred head of cattle. There is little or no evidence cattle from Texas were driven to Sedalia in the so-called "Rawhide" era immediately after the Civil War. If any arrived, they were few in number. In the twentieth century the railroad built a stockyard on the Lexington Branch west of Park Avenue in northwest Sedalia.

The MK&T stockyard, established prior to 1876, was on approximately fifty acres between Clinton Road and the Katy mainline. Valued at $25,000 in 1896, it was served by two spurs and handled large shipments of cattle from Texas, Indian Territory (later Oklahoma), and Kansas, many on the way to Chicago packing houses. The Katy stockyard served as a livestock auction barn after World War II until abandoned in 1954 shortly before the adjacent Katy shops were closed.

Union Depot at Third and Engineer was shared by the Missouri Pacific and MK&T between 1872 and 1877. In 1877 the Garrison House became the Union Depot, serving in that capacity until it burned in 1885. Then the Missouri Pacific built a two-story depot of brick and Warrensburg stone trim at a cost of $35,000 on the site of the Garrison House. The Katy shared these quarters until its new depot opened for business in 1896 on East Third Street. The Missouri Pacific depot had separate waiting rooms for ladies and gentlemen and a lobby with imported French floor tiling. The second floor housed the offices of the division superintendent and other officials. In a misguided attempt to "modernize" the depot, the railroad removed the second floor in the early 1950s, and otherwise "streamlined" the building.

The Katy's new depot opened May 10, 1896. Cost overruns pushed the cost to over $40,000. Ironically, it opened the same week the railroad announced an $800,000 cost-cutting campaign, including eliminating some Katy Flyers and laying off workers. The two-story depot is 32 by 205 feet with floor space of 10,785 square feet. Constructed of pressed brick with Carthage stone trim, the ground floor had, besides ticket and express offices and baggage and waiting rooms, a dining room, lunch stand, and newsstand. The second floor housed division offices. The dining room opened May 10 under the supervision of M. L. Oglesby. Located in the center of the building with doors on east and west sides, it was finished in "massive" oak with a painted tin ceiling and furnished with square tables seating eight. The menu opening day included soup and boiled lake trout with cream sauce; meat and vegetables; roast turkey and dressing; fruits, nuts, and strawberries; and ice cream with cake and coffee. Trains No. 2 and No. 3 stopped for breakfast; No. 1 and No. 4 stopped for supper. The

Above, left: Firemen's training was poor in the nineteenth century, prompting Major William Beck to make his famous suggestion that Sedalia's firemen practice three days before every fire. (Ed Brummet Collection)

Above, right: The Clay and Heynen Marble Works was located at the northwest corner of North Ohio and Pacific Streets, just east of the Lamy Manufacturing Company. C. H. Heynen joined C. C. Clay in 1876 and became a partner in 1881, not long before this picture was taken. Heynen later bought out Clay and moved the monument business to the northeast corner of Third and Massachusetts Streets. (Ed Brummet Collection)

Lake Creek Methodist Church, five miles south of Smithton, has hosted camp meetings since 1843. This building was constructed in 1883. (Ed Brummet Collection)

lunchroom was open all night. This depot was one of the finest in the entire Katy system, and, after decades of neglect, is scheduled for restoration by the State of Missouri in 1998. (It is an important link in the trans-Missouri Katy Trail.)

The 1880s were a time of national labor unrest, manifested in Sedalia by railroad strikes. Labor had been watching in resentment as "greedy" capitalists concentrated wealth and power in their hands. At the same time, management was cutting wages, lengthening work hours, and discharging longtime employees without explanation. The first local strike grew out of a temperance "riot" in July 1877. Temperance rallies sometimes grew quite fervent, and this one metamorphosed into a strike against the Katy for three months' back pay, among other grievances. It was settled a week later on terms favorable to the strikers. In 1880, Missouri Pacific shop mechanics demanded wage increases; management refused, closed the shops, and fired the strikers.

On March 7, 1885, workers at both shops and elsewhere went on strike, halting trains on the entire Gould system from Missouri to Texas. The railroad asked Governor John S. Marmaduke to send state militia to Sedalia to break the strike. However, a delegation of Sedalia businessmen and strikers met with the governor and asked him not to send troops; he decided in their favor. A week later the railroads submitted to the demands of the strikers. The last strike, in 1886, was precipitated by the firing of a Knights of Labor official by the Texas Pacific in Texas. This time there was vandalism and sabotage of railroad property in Sedalia, including a derailment resulting in four injuries. The strikers had neither support nor sympathy from Sedalia's business community and citizens. Armed protection was furnished for strikers who wanted to return to

Above: The sawmill on the right is powered by the steam engine on the left, which seems to be in a hole. (Ed Brummet Collection)

Top of page: Note what appears to be a steam engine in front of the A. F. Neumeyer Hardware Store in Smithton. The Neumeyers operated several businesses in Smithton. (Verona Neumeyer Collection)

Above: The butchers at J. G. Kehl's pose in their shop with their equipment and fresh meat. Note the telephones on extreme right. Sedalia had two telephone companies, the Home and the Bell, for many years until Southwestern Bell secured the sole franchise. (Ed Brummet Collection)

Facing page, above: The J. G. Kehl Meat Market proudly exhibits a beef raised in Pettis County by N. H. Gentry. The meat market was in the old city hall. (Ed Brummet Collection)

Missouri north of the Missouri River. Sedalia liked to point out that Jefferson City's railroad connections touched only twenty-two counties, while Sedalia's connections touched fifty-four, including counties north of the river. In its April 28, 1896 edition, the *Sedalia Capital* said:

> *Goodness knows the 67-year-old town does no honor to Jefferson. There is no Missourian or American who has ever visited Monticello, the home of Jefferson, in Va., that would think for a moment that Jefferson City, Mo., ever did him any credit, and Jefferson would be really honored by removing the capital from "Sleepy Hollow" . . . [Jefferson City] has been notorious for 40 years and more as one of the sickliest localities for a town in Missouri.*

Above: Jesse Swope and his wife Nannie Lower, right, lived on their 200-acre farm in Longwood Township. The first polls in what became Pettis County were at Mr. Swope's father's home a mile northeast of this farmhouse, long gone. (Rich Mewes Collection)

Right: Jesse and Nancy (Lower) Swope were married in Pettis County in 1859 and eventually had ten children. They lived on their farm southwest of Longwood from 1867 until their deaths over fifty years later. Jesse's sister Sarah (Sallie) was reportedly the first white woman born in what became Pettis County, and her marriage to Nathaniel Newhill on March 28, 1833, was the second one recorded in Pettis County. (The first marriage was two days earlier.) (Rich Mewes Collection)

Above, left: The 100 block of West Main on the north side is temporarily deserted. The stores are, left to right, W. E. Bard Drug Company, People's Furniture Store, Dan Wilcox Drug Store (Dr. Staats upstairs), and John Brandt Groceries (U.S. Army Recruiting Station upstairs). (Ed Brummet Collection)

Above, right: Henry Jones of Heath Creek Township built this house in 1878 on his 670-acre farm near Newland. Remnants of the old Osage Trail, later Arrow Rock–Osceola Road, can be seen on this farm, now owned by Mr. Jones' grandson, Van G. Jones and his wife, Betty Bob. (William B. Claycomb Collection)

Top of page: John W. Menefee livery, feed, and sales stables were located at 401 West Main Street, Sedalia. With the advent of automobiles, the livery business declined, although Mr. Menefee and his son remained in the horse sales business for several years after the turn of the century. (Ed Brummet Collection)

The old city hall at the southwest corner of Second and Osage Streets was built in 1874 and served the city for almost a century. (Pettis County Historical Society Collection)

Honorable John H. Bothwell and Senator Charles E. Yeater of Pettis County sponsored Concurrent Resolution No. 20 that passed both houses of the General Assembly February 20, 1895. This resolution submitted to the qualified voters of Missouri a proposed amendment to the Constitution "providing for the removal of the seat of government from Jefferson City to Sedalia, and also providing for the donation of grounds to the state and for the erection thereon without expense to the state, of a capitol building, a supreme court building, armory, and executive mansion equal or superior in area, stability, and architectural merit to the buildings now owned by the state at Jefferson City." The buildings were to be ready for occupancy November 1, 1899, unless an extension was granted for good cause. Sedalia was also to bear the cost of moving the state's records and property.

Professional appraisers estimated that it would cost $594,204 to replace the state's current buildings and $10,000 for land. The land was available—a beautiful tract of some 240 acres south of Sixteenth Street, north of the Katy tracks, and west of what later became South Limit. And, on May 1, 1896, Sedalia filed a $600,000 performance bond with Governor Joel Stone

There was a street light in the middle of Main and Ohio at the turn of the century. The U.S. Army Recruiting Office is in the second floor office on the left. The third floor and bay windows are gone today. (Pettis County Historical Society Collection)

to guarantee the erection of the new buildings without cost to the state if the removal amendment met with voter approval. Twenty-four Sedalia businessmen—most if not all were members of the Sedalia Board of Trade—signed personal bonds to back the $600,000 bond.

An architect was engaged to draw plans for the proposed capitol. He designed a magnificent building 420 feet long, 200 feet deep in the middle, and 100 feet deep in the wings. It was to be 68 feet high to the base of the dome, and 125 feet to the top. It was to be in the "Ionic and French Renaissance style of architecture," what we today would call Beaux-Arts; be built of gray sandstone and granite; and be four stories including the basement. The interior was to be finished in marble and Missouri onyx, and the ceilings decorated with frescoes and plaster with reliefs.

The *Sedalia Capital*, which appears to have been the Board of Trade's mouthpiece, promoted the removal scheme ceaselessly for a year. In the end, Sedalia's efforts failed. The November 3, 1896, vote was:

Colonel A. D. Jaynes and Cyrus Newkirk founded the First National Bank, Pettis County's first bank, in 1866. It was on the northwest corner of Second and Ohio Streets, the building on the right in this picture. It went into bankruptcy in 1894. The Sedalia Drug Company is on the ground floor, left. (Pettis County Historical Society Collection)

For removal	181,258	35.1%
Against removal	334,819	64.9%
	516,077	100.0%

Pettis County itself voted 7,284 to 632 for removal, as did Jackson County at 20,883 to 8,931. Cole County, home of Jefferson City, not surprisingly turned it down 4,115 to 44. St. Louis City also decisively turned it down 67,131 to 25,080. In all, only sixteen counties, mostly bordering Pettis and to its west, voted for removal. Ninety-eight counties and the city of St. Louis voted against the proposition.

Once the *Sedalia Capital* accepted the embarrassing defeat, it headlined "Let Us Build Factories" and suggested that a $500,000 bond issue be used to capitalize a Sedalia Improvement Company. Nothing came of this at first, but a few years into the new century factories were built, but they were called railroad shops. In addition, Sedalia was to be given a consolation prize for losing the state capital: the Missouri State Fair.

Sedalia's arguments to be capital had merit, and the proffered capitol site was splendid. But the cost of removal would have been a heavy and longtime burden on local taxpayers who had only recently paid off the county's railroad bonds.

QUEEN CITY

Trunk Factory!

Manufacturer of and Dealer in all kinds of

Sample, Packing and Traveling TRUNKS, VALISES, SATCHELS, and Baskets.

Trunks and Valises Repaired. Old Trunks and Valises Taken in Exchange.

J. RAUTENSTRAUCH.

225 Ohio St. Next to Sicher's.

RATES $1. **RATES $1.**

RILEY'S HOTEL,

212 & 214 West Second Street,

Opposite Market Square.

Come see MR. RILEY who keeps the hotel.
He's a jolly old soul, and will use you right well,
His tables are spread with the best in the land;
When anything is wanted, he's right at your hand.

His beds are first-class, the best in the town;
Now this is a fact, for I've been all around.
Now, drummers, come try him, he'll use you right well,
For he's MR. RILEY who keeps the hotel.

Weekly Board at Low Rates

W. B. RILEY, - Proprietor.

Above, left: Judge E. W. Washburn (1814–1899), presiding judge of the postwar Radical Republican Pettis County Court, and his colleagues issued bonds to assist railroad construction. Washburn and his daughter, Mrs. J. D. Claycomb, were the first school teachers in Sedalia and he was the first president of the school board in 1866. He later taught school and served as justice of the peace at Thornleigh, north of Sedalia. (William B. Claycomb Collection)

Above, right: Dr. John W. Trader (1837–1907) was Surgeon of the Second Regiment, Missouri National Guard, with the rank of major. After distinguished service in the Union Army as a surgeon during the Civil War, he practiced medicine and surgery in Sedalia for forty years. He held many offices, including that of president of the Missouri Medical Association. Dr. Charles B. Trader was one of his eight children. (Ed Brummet Collection)

Above: Julius Rautenstrauch, owner of the Queen City Trunk Factory, came to Sedalia in 1878. He had three sons—Alfred; Irwin, who shortened his surname to Raut; and Walter (1880–1951), who became famous as professor of industrial engineering at Columbia University (New York) in the 1920s and father of the short-lived Technocracy Movement in the 1930s. Walter founded the first Department of Industrial Engineering in the country at Columbia in 1919. (Ed Brummet Collection)

Many Pettis Countians still have fond memories of the Flat Creek covered bridge. Built in 1881, vandals burned it in the spring of 1966. (Ed Brummet Collection)

This magnificent round barn on Green Ridge Road southwest of Sedalia had fallen on hard times by 1960. It was destroyed by a storm shortly after this picture was taken. (Ed Brummet Collection)

Above: The 200 block of South Ohio was busy in the 1890s. The St. Louis Clothing Company is on the left. (Ed Brummet Collection)

Facing page, above, left: B. F. Prigmore built this house three miles northwest of Houstonia circa 1880. Mr. and Mrs. Clay Parsons, the current owners, have restored it, using woodwork and other architectural features salvaged from nearby Avondale, the magnificent 1880 house built for Thomas B. Price and demolished about 1980. (Ed Brummet Collection)

Facing page, above, right: The J. H. Mertz home was at 209 East Broadway. Mr. Mertz was a prominent Sedalia druggist whose store was at 210 South Ohio. (Pettis County Historical Society Collection)

Facing page, below: The Benton H. Ingram house was located on what is now the Bothwell Hospital block. Ingram came to Sedalia in 1864 and engaged in the retail and insurance business. He also served as Pettis County collector and circuit clerk. Mr. and Mrs. Ingram had five children, including two sons, Martin and Charles, who are probably the boys in the yard and on the tricycle in this 1880s picture. (Ed Brummet Collection)

E. B. Herndon Fine Groceries at 608 South Ohio offered home delivery service. The "delivery boys" depended on their horses to get them around town. The Story and Clark Piano Company is next door at 606 South Ohio. (Ed Brummet Collection)

Before there was Dorn-Cloney Laundry, there was Bowman and Dorn Steam Laundry. The building appears to be the Katy freight depot on East Main Street. (Ed Brummet Collection)

What we now know as the Missouri Pacific Depot was the Union Depot from 1885 to 1896, serving not only the Missouri Pacific and its branch lines to Lexington and Warsaw, but also the Katy Railroad. The train in this old photograph could be either a MoPac or Katy train. The second floor was removed in the early 1950s. (Ed Brummet Collection)

Chief of Police Tom Prentiss is standing in the left door of this Romanesque building in the 200 block of East Third Street, still used by Home Lumber Company. The Huckins, later Terry, Hotel can be glimpsed in the background on East Second Street. (Ed Brummet Collection)

The well-dressed Broadway School freshman English class walked a block east to pose for this picture in front of the D. H. Smith mansion on June 3, 1890. The Smith house was in the 100 block of West Broadway on the north side of the street. (Ed Brummet Collection)

A flower-decorated carriage passes by in the "prosperity" parade. The driver and his escort on horseback are in uniform; the ladies are dressed in their finest attire. (Ed Brummet Collection)

The parade has come to a standstill. These fashionably dressed ladies' float promotes "prosperity." The large building in the background is not identified. (Ed Brummet Collection)

Above and left: The barns on Oakdale Farm are significant for their size, interior design, and preservation. Major William Gentry (1818–1890) made most of the improvements to Oakdale, his showplace home farm. (William B. Claycomb Collection)

Above, left: This Sedalia landmark at 705 West Sixth Street was built for Joseph Imhauser in 1895. Henry W. Harris, prominent banker, bought it in 1898 and it remained in his family for seventy years. It is on the National Register of Historic Places. (Ed Brummet Collection)

Above, right: Sedalia was host to the 1892 Missouri Bankers Association convention. O. A. Crandall organized the Missouri Trust Company in 1880; by 1892 it was the Sedalia National Bank, left. It closed in bankruptcy in 1932 after Charles Evans, t he managing officer and Mr.Crandall's son-in-law, killed himself. (Pettis County Historical Society Collection)

Right: Had the voters of Missouri voted in favor of removing the capital to Sedalia in 1896, this is the capitol building Sedalia and Pettis County were going to provide the state. It would have been located on what are now the state fair grounds. (William B. Claycomb Collection)

Below: Baldwin Locomotive Works built MK&T "camel back" engine No. 251 in 1895. It was later rebuilt with conventional boilers and renumbered No. 613. (Kehde's Barbeque Collection)

Chapter Four

Above: Detail of Muddy Creek.

Left: Honorable John H. Bothwell enjoyed canoeing on Muddy Creek below the lodge. This scenic spot is now an unsightly slough. (Pettis County Historical Society Collection)

Above, left: The orator in the center of the picture has drawn a large and festive crowd around his platform at Main and Ohio Streets. This view looks southeast toward the Citizens National Bank. (Ed Brummet Collection)

Above, right: This picture was probably taken the same day as the one at left and shows a throng at West Main and Osage Streets, looking southwest. An elaborate stage has been erected across Main Street. (Ed Brummet Collection)

Pettis County's newly freed blacks went in different directions after the Civil War. Some left their old homes and were able to buy lots in places like Dresden. Others moved to Sedalia or out of the county. Still others stayed on at the homes of their former owners. In 1870, eight blacks, all named Fristoe, lived with Pettis County pioneer Amos Fristoe in Longwood Township. Fristoe left one young black man five acres when he died in 1872. Ten blacks and one mulatto lived in the Joseph Cartwright household in nearby Heath's Creek Township. There were also several black families living on or near the large Cartwright farm. Other blacks were scattered throughout the county, serving as laborers and "domestic servants."

The largest black neighborhood was called Colorado Black Settlement, located on Heath's Creek three miles west of Longwood. In 1880 fourteen families lived on small farms in the Heath's Creek hills. There were seventy-six blacks in the settlement, including sixteen classified as mulatto. The men were farmers, the women kept house, and the children were "at school." The Zion Methodist Episcopal Church served the community. But by about 1890 the settlement had mysteriously vanished and was soon forgotten. These people left behind only their enumeration in the 1880 census.

The plight of blacks who moved to urban areas was expressed by a young man in *The Buffalo Express*, and reprinted in the *Sedalia Daily Capital* Saturday, February 6, 1897.

Above: This is the last train on the old narrow gauge Sedalia, Warsaw, and Southwestern Railroad leaving Sedalia on August 3, 1902. The "Warsaw Branch" was subsequently converted to standard gauge and abandoned shortly after World War II. (Pettis County Historical Society Collection)

Top of page: These young Sedalia men were in Company D, Second Regiment, Missouri Volunteer Infantry at the time of the Spanish-American War in 1898. Corporal Edward L. Hardin is second from left. They never left the U.S. (Ed Brummet Collection)

These men broke ground for the new Missouri Pacific shops in east Sedalia on May 10, 1904. Note the lady in her white dress among the men on the right. (Pettis County Historical Society Collection)

> *We suffer, not at the hands of the moneyed power, that you have heard so much about recently, but at the hands of the laboring people. It is impossible for a negro to obtain other positions than those of the barber, porter, plasterer or domestic servant, because none of the other branches of labor are open to him. The railroads, the greatest industrial organization on the continent, employ in the northern states over 500,000 men, and yet there is but one position, that of car porter, open to the negro, owing to the influence of the many labor organizations that will not let negroes into their societies or work with them in any other position.*

The same newspaper reported that Robert Morton, a young "negro" of Rockfield, Kentucky, was shot then hanged by a mob for writing "an insulting and insinuating note to Miss Tommis Johnson, a popular young white woman . . . " On May 1, 1903, J. Elbert Cutter publicized the results of a survey he conducted on lynchings in the United States from 1882 to 1903. In that period he recorded 3,128 lynchings, including 61 women. One thousand eight hundred and seventy-two (sixty percent) were black, and 1,256 (forty percent) were white. Fifty-four percent of the lynchings took place in the South, and thirty-five percent were for black "crimes" against women, such as Robert Morton's alleged crime against Miss Johnson. The only known black lynching in Pettis County occurred in 1853 in Georgetown when a young slave was burned alive for the axe-murder of a white woman in Longwood Township. He was apparently encouraged to commit the crime by his master, who was forced to leave the county prior to the lynching.

In the fall of 1893, one of the jewels in the Queen City's crown arrived in the person of a black itinerant pianist named Scott Joplin. In January 1894, the George R. Smith College for blacks opened. Built and operated by the Freedmen's Aid Society of the Methodist Episcopal Church, the approximately twenty-five-acre campus had been donated by General Smith's daughters, Martha Smith and Sarah Cotton. Located in northeast Sedalia west of Crown Hill Cemetery, the city had bypassed this land and, a century later, it is still undeveloped. In 1896 Joplin, who had been coming to and going from Sedalia, enrolled in the college to study harmony and composition. The next year he wrote the "Maple Leaf Rag," although it was not published until 1899 when it sold seventy-five thousand copies the first six months. Having outgrown Sedalia, John Stark, Joplin's publisher, moved to St. Louis in 1900 and Joplin followed later that year. Both St. Louis and Sedalia claim to be the Cradle of Ragtime, but Sedalia has the better claim, even though it did not go out of its way at the time to support Joplin or nourish his music. The college burned to the ground on April 26, 1925, and having lost the support of the Methodist Church, it closed May 5.

This pair of pictures shows a watermelon stand at the northwest corner of the courthouse square, looking northwest toward the Missouri Trust Building. Street fairs seem to have been popular in turn-of-the-century Sedalia. (Ed Brummet Collection)

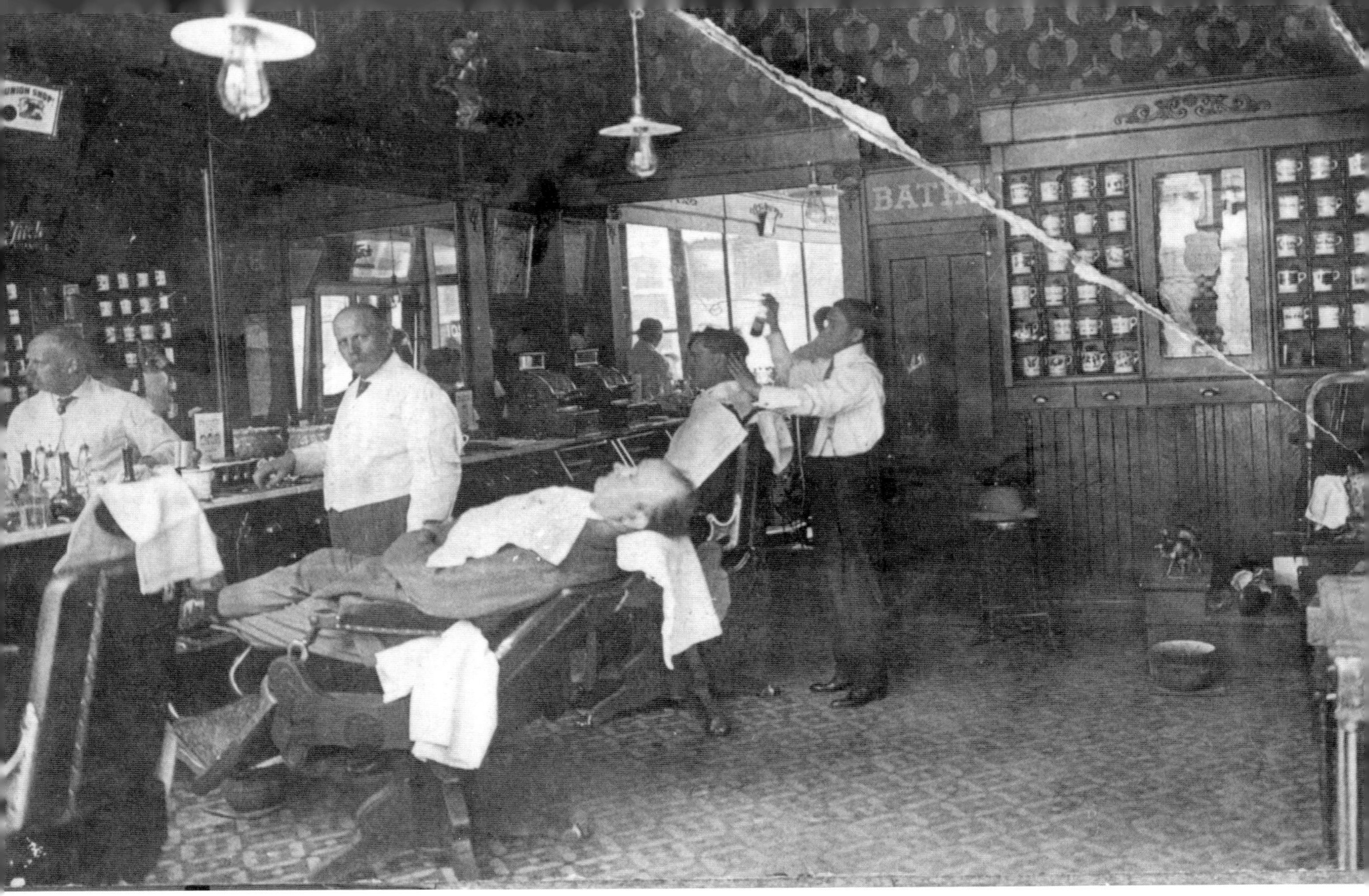

Turn-of-the-century barber shops offered haircuts, shaves, shoeshines, and baths. Note customers' personal shaving mugs in the cabinet on the right. (Joe Henry Martin Collection)

Sedalia's population in 1900 was 15,231; that of the county was 32,438. Sedalia ranked sixth in the state after St. Louis, Kansas City, St. Joseph, Springfield, and Joplin—a ranking it held for decades. The city's first major event of the new century was its selection as the home of the Missouri State Fair. Thanks to John Bothwell, Charles Yeater, and Nicholas Gentry, among others, the first fair was held in 1901 on the ground previously offered for the capitol. Sedalia architect Thomas W. Bast (1863–1933) was engaged to design permanent buildings, a commission he admirably fulfilled. He designed all the buildings up to 1926, the Administration Building being his last. All are still in service.

In 1898 the Katy moved its shops to new quarters one mile southwest of the Fifth and Hancock site. The new shops were built on a 118-acre tract south of Twentieth Street, north of the mainline, and east of Limit. It was served by ten spurs off the mainline. The largest of the principal buildings covered some three acres; three others were an acre in size. Peak employment of 898 was reached in World War I, then declined for forty years. In 1924 the Katy shops became a car shop; closed during the depression; reopened, but finally closed for good October 15, 1957. The shops were dismantled and demolished in 1962. By that time the Katy's

Mrs. John Armstrong is reported to have been the first woman driver in Sedalia. Here she is shown "on" the family automobile, stick in hand, with Mr. Armstrong. (Ed Brummet Collection)

Andrew Carnegie gave Sedalia $50,000 in 1900 to construct one of the finest Carnegie Libraries in Missouri. He was ready to give Sedalia an additional $4,000 to landscape the half block when he received a letter from a local labor leader denouncing him and his money. The $4,000 offer was subsequently withdrawn. (Sedalia Public Library Collection)

Sedalia lost the capital in 1896, but gained the State Fair in 1901. George E. Kessler, a prominent Kansas City landscape designer, designed the Missouri State Fair grounds. Sedalia architect Thomas Bast designed all the fair's brick buildings in an eclectic style. (Sedalia Public Library Collection)

once-beautiful depot had been leased to and remodeled by the Boeing Company, the prime contractor for the Minuteman Missile Complex headquartered at Whiteman Air Force Base, eighteen miles west of Sedalia.

Meanwhile, the Missouri Pacific Railroad, who already employed between five hundred and seven hundred men in its shops on 20 acres east of Engineer Street north of the mainline, was making a major decision. In 1903 it announced the railroad would consolidate the line's shops. Railroad officials informed Sedalia that it would qualify as a candidate for the prize if it offered them 125 acres east of the old shops worth $25,000, plus a $200,000 cash bonus. And this $225,000 bid was not a guaranty Sedalia would get the shops. Other cities wanted them, in particular Atchison, Kansas, and Kansas City. Sedalia eventually beat the stiff competition with some inside-the-board-room help. The shops were secured in 1904 and built in 1905, reportedly the largest car and locomotive repair shops west of the Mississippi River. The ten principal buildings were served by at least fifteen spur lines from the mainline. The Missouri Pacific employed up to fourteen hundred men before the great 1922 strike, excluding employees at the depot, division and freight offices, and on rolling stock. Demand for labor was so great the railroad at times imported it. In 1910 a hundred Bulgarians worked at the shops. The young men lived together in a colony near the shops for several years before returning to their homeland when World War I broke out. (Bulgaria was an ally of Germany.) Like the Katy, employment and operations steadily declined after the 1922 strike until only a small signal shop remained by the 1980s.

The Missouri Pacific (now the Union Pacific Railroad) still owns 205 acres altogether in Sedalia, including what is left of the shops, switching yards, and right-of-way. After the railroad abandoned this property, Sedalia officials, remembering it had been given to the railroad in 1904, asked for half of it back for industrial park development. The Union Pacific refused.

Pettis County's statewide reputation for leadership in agriculture dates from the so-called Golden Age of Agriculture (1909–1914). It was during this time, also called the Age of Parity, that Pettis County's famous livestock breeders were in their prime. Nicholas H. Gentry (1850–1933) of Cedar Township was the country's foremost Berkshire hog breeder and prominent Shorthorn cattle breeder. Colonel L. M. Monsees (1858–1947) of Bowling Green Township was the nation's foremost jack breeder, largely responsible for the famous Missouri mule. And N. C. McFarland (1867–1946), also of Bowling Green Township, was the state's best known Duroc-Jersey hog breeder. These remarkable stockmen had the 1904 St. Louis World's Fair grand championship trophies to support their reputations.

They were active and successful in public affairs as well. Mr. Gentry served on the State Board of Agriculture for about twenty-five years, as well as the State Fair Board. He was a director of the American Shorthorn Breeders' Association and American Berkshire Breeders' Association. He was Missouri Commissioner for the 1893 Chicago World's Fair and the 1904 St. Louis Fair, the only Missourian to serve both fairs; and he was an adviser to World War I Food Administrator Herbert Hoover. He was also president of the American Royal Live Stock Show and served on its board for twenty-five years.

Longwood was the earliest town in what became Pettis County. The settlement was originally just north of the present location and was a stop on a stagecoach route. In this early twentieth century photograph, the Hoffman store is on the left and a blacksmith shop is on the right. The store building remains. (Ruby K. Schondelmeyer Collection)

Pettis County built many iron bridges early in the century. This one is on Heath Creek north of Longwood. Most if not all of the iron bridges have been replaced. (Ruby K. Schondelmeyer Collection)

shops kept up a deafening clamor all day. Street cars were clanging over 8.25 miles of track every ten to twenty minutes. The town was heated by coal and wood, and from late fall to early spring smoke and soot cast a pall over the city. Horse manure littered the streets, although automobiles were replacing horses as the 1910 decade got under way. Untreated sewage flowed by gravity into Flat and Muddy Creeks until 1916.

On the other hand, Sedalia enjoyed excellent water, school, and park systems. Liberty Park boasted a convention hall built in 1911 that compared favorably with facilities in much larger cities. The busy T. W. Bast was architect. Regrettably his building was spoiled fifty years later when the front porch loggia and side porte-cochere were removed and the half-moon Palladian auditorium windows bricked up. Sedalia was also the entertainment center for west central Missouri. Entertainments ranged from spectacles at the Woods Opera House and vaudeville at the Sedalia Theater, to somewhat less enlightening diversions on Main Street.

When the United States declared war on Germany and its allies in April 1917, Pettis Countians responded to the call to service with patriotic fervor: 2,850 people, almost all men, went into uniform during the nine-

Claude and Chester Karrick of Longwood pose in their wagon made by J. R. Marcum of Hughesville. Their brother Jackson sits atop one of the mules. (Ruby K. Schondelmeyer Collection)

In this picture of Longwood Dr. J. D. Prowell's house is on the left, the Hoffman store beyond it. The two-story building in the rear housed the Modern Woodmen on the second floor. By-passed by the railroads and good roads, Longwood never enjoyed significant growth. (Ruby K. Schondelmeyer Collection)

Longwood School was typical of rural Pettis County schools. On October 29, 1907, forty-one pupils and one teacher came to school. High school was out of reach for most rural families, at least until after World War I. (Pettis County Historical Society Collection)

teen months the country was at war. This was approximately 17 percent of the total male population. Probably a majority never got out of the country, but a substantial minority did, and ended up in French trenches. Fifty-three died, some in action, others of the influenza epidemic and other diseases. The handful of women who volunteered, estimated at a dozen, served mostly as nurses.

On the home front, Pettis Countians (as well as the rest of the country) were under constant pressure from the U.S. Treasury to buy Liberty Bonds to finance the war. Quotas were set for the four principal campaigns, chairmen were appointed, propaganda and peer pressure employed, and quotas were met. Even children were not exempt. They were assigned a quota and encouraged to buy "Baby Bonds." In all, the Treasury sold about $4,500,000 worth of bonds to Pettis Countians.

In 1919 most of the soldiers came home, marched in a great parade downtown, disbanded, and packed their uniforms away. Meanwhile, the politicians were meeting in Paris and making a vindictive peace that proved to be only a twenty-year cease-fire.

Above: The Bealert Hotel in Hughesville was in an odd semi-adobe style. In front, circa 1908, left to right are: R. E. Bealert, C. D. Mockbee, Henry Martin, Dave Ebersole, and unidentified. The Bealerts operated the hotel and restaurant for fifty years. (Joe Henry Martin Collection)

Left: Automobiles had made their appearance in Hughesville by 1916. The Bealert family operated the hotel at left center and the general merchandise store on the right. The stockyards, R. T. Bealert Store, and garage are gone, but most of the center block remains. (Joe Henry Martin Collection)

Above, left: This building served as the Hughesville High School between World War I and World War II. Today Northwest High School occupies this site just north of Hughesville. (Joe Henry Martin Collection)

Above, right: Hughesville was a major shipping point for fat cattle for two generations before World War II. The area was ideally suited to cattle feeding and fortunes were made, and lost, in the business. This is a view of the stockyards and downtown Hughesville December 29, 1907. (Joe Henry Martin Collection)

On Wednesday afternoon, June 16, 1920, three "tinners" employed by the Ilgenfritz Hardware Company were replacing the tin sheeting on the courthouse roof. The men, A. W. Meyer, William Creegan, and Joseph Esser, were working in the vicinity of the base of the dome. Mr. Meyer climbed up the side of the dome and when just below the cupola, he discovered that the dome, made of wood, was ablaze. (Unlike the rest of the structure, which was constructed of stone veneer, the dome was made of wood, reportedly because the county ran short of money in 1884 and the contractor, who supposedly lost $25,000 on the contract anyway, was allowed to substitute wood for stone in the tower.) The workmen, who had been using blowtorches the week before, denied that they had used any the day of the fire. At any rate, the dome caught fire around 3:30 P.M. and the dry wood burned quickly. Meyer escaped through the burning building. The other two men could not reach the roof exit and eventually lowered themselves to the ground by means of a rope. Meanwhile the occupants of the courthouse's second floor were unaware of the fire until Superintendent of County Schools T. R. Luckett and others looked out their windows and saw burning chunks of the dome falling over the side of the building. By that time the second floor was on fire and the county officeholders made a narrow escape. There were no serious injuries and with the help of the public almost all of the county records were saved. Blowing embers from the fire started a dozen roof fires on East Fourth and Fifth Streets. The county had $55,000 insurance on the

$100,000 building, $5,000 on the contents, and $800 on the clock.

The next day Judge Henry Lamm, who, as prosecuting attorney in 1884, served on the new courthouse advisory committee, described the courthouse as "the best in Central Missouri, and the first of its kind. Everybody was proud of it when it was built and so far as I know, has been proud of it ever since for it was really and truly an honestly built and fine building."

Built at a cost of $100,000 after a vigorous campaign over the opposition of many who did not wish to issue another $100,000 in bonds on top of all the railroad bonds the county was obligated for, the two-story building was 100 by 145 feet with a tower and lantern, and four corner pavilions. It sat on a raised ten-foot foundation of Carthage stone over a basement. The two courtrooms on the second floor were richly decorated with wall frescoes and painted ceilings; the oak furniture was hand carved.

It is unlikely Judge Lamm or anyone else would have guessed it would be five years before Pettis County would have a new courthouse.

Sunnymede School was located three miles southwest of Longwood on the William Lower farm. It was absorbed into the Longwood C-3 District in 1935, which was itself consolidated into the Hughesville RV District in 1964. This building survived until the early 1990s. (Pettis County Historical Society Collection)

Above: The Smithton Auto Company seems to have shared quarters with a real estate firm in the 1910s. (Verona Neumeyer Collection)

Facing page, above: Miss Lucy Hopkins, teacher of the Prairie Valley School No. 40, four miles northeast of Hughesville on the John McClure farm, leads her pupils in exercise in 1904. Note the large picture of Jesus on the rear wall. (Rich Mewes Collection)

Facing page, below: Miss Lucy Hopkins and her twenty pupils pose outside Prairie Valley School the same day of the inside picture above. (Note the girls' dresses are the same in both pictures.) Married women could not teach in Missouri prior to World War II. Once married, a woman's teaching career was over. (Rich Mewes Collection)

Above, left: Turn-of-the-century young ladies, if their families could afford it, often had formal photographs made prior to marriage. Ella Waldecker of Hughesville is wearing her best dress and proudly displaying her long hair in this photograph. Her father, Edward H. Waldecker, owned an 80-acre farm five miles northeast of Hughesville at the junction of U.S. 65 and Route D. (Rich Mewes Collection)

Above, right: Ella Waldecker, left, and friends had their picture taken in a St. Louis studio, possibly at the 1904 World's Fair. Note the painted backdrop but authentic-looking "auto-carriage." Miss Waldecker married Jesse Wheeler of Hughesville, grandson of Jesse Swope. (Rich Mewes Collection)

The old Sedalia Masonic Lodge stood on the southwest corner of Seventh and Osage. It was originally the Cumberland Presbyterian Church, but it was purchased and remodeled by the Masonic Lodge in 1906–1907. It served as the Masonic home for over fifty years. Today it is a private parking lot. (Ed Brummet Collection)

Facing page, above, left: The house of A. F. Neumeyer, prominent Smithton businessman, is typical of the frame houses built by prosperous families late in the nineteenth and early twentieth centuries. (Verona Neumeyer Collection)

Facing page, above, right: This is thought to be the general store in Smithton early in the century. The proprietor offered canned goods, potatoes, graham crackers (to his left), and lots of rope and twine (on his right), among other merchandise. (Pettis County Historical Society Collection)

Above: The Sedalia Country Club was founded in 1905 on the state fairgrounds. That location proved unsatisfactory, and in 1910 the club purchased a fifty-eight-acre tract south of the fair beyond the Katy tracks and improved it with a nine-hole golf course and this clubhouse. All but three of the twenty-nine ladies seem to be wearing the same dress in this photograph. (Ed Brummet Collection)

Right: The old First Christian Church, southwest corner of Seventh and Massachusetts, was dedicated in 1889 and served its congregation for seventy-five years. When a new church was built in 1964, the property was sold to the Sedalia Democrat Company which razed the church to make way for the new "Democrat" building. (Ed Brummet Collection)

Above: This picture of an engine and workmen was taken at the Missouri Pacific shops about 1912. By this time the shops were so big and labor so short that management imported Bulgarians to work. The Bulgarians went home when World War I broke out and fought on the side of the Germans. (Pettis County Historical Society Collection)

Left: This Katy train derailed in Sedalia June 20, 1908. The engine is on its side on the left, the coal tender in the center. (Ed Brummet Collection)

Above: A dirigible powered by a propeller flies above The Ruralist tent at the Missouri State Fair grounds circa 1910. The demonstration drew a large crowd. (Pettis County Historical Society Collection)

Left: The Katy Building is under construction at 219–223 South Ohio. E. G. Cassidy built this building and named it after his wife, not the railroad. It is remembered as the long-time home of the C. W. Flower Company and has been covered with a false front for decades. (Ed Brummet Collection)

Below: The 1910–1911 fourth grade class of Broadway School gathered for a class picture. Miss Creagan was the teacher; Miss Grace Collins was the art teacher. Today's Third National Bank is on the old Broadway School block. (Ed Brummet Collection)

Above: Sedalia improved Liberty Park in the second decade of the twentieth century. The improvements included an impressive convention hall and landscaping projects. The lagoon's island, dating from the 1890s, remains one of the city's picturesque spots. (Sedalia Public Library Collection)

Top of page: Sedalia's horse-drawn fire engines were finally replaced with a fire truck in 1914. Mayor Fred L. Ludemann (beside the driver) and a dozen passengers, mostly young women, took a ride in front of Pettis County's splendid courthouse. (Sedalia Public Library Collection)

Above, left: President William Howard Taft (in the back seat) arrives at the Missouri State Fair grandstand in October 1911, in E. G. Cassidy's car. The president was accompanied by Congressman John T. Heard of Sedalia. A year later President Taft was defeated for reelection by Woodrow Wilson. (Pettis County Historical Society Collection)

Above, right: A. M. Parks's Sedalia Egg Company, a wholesale fruit and produce firm, was located at 105–107 East Main Street, Sedalia. His delivery truck appears to have been steered from the right. (Pettis County Historical Society Collection)

Top of page: This large group of Smithton men and their numbered dogs were fox and wolf hunting at Elk Lick Spring in May 1911. Elk Lick was a resort in southeast Saline County just north of the Pettis County line. (Pettis County Historical Society Collection)

Pettis County fox hunters have pitched their tents to camp out for the night. Colonel L. M. Monsees is fifth man from right. Fox hunting was a popular sport prior to World War I. (Pettis County Historical Society Collection)

Colonel L. M. Monsees is standing in shirtsleeves in front of the speaker's platform at what is reported to be a fox hunt on June 4, 1914. Colonel Monsees was at the height of his fame as the country's foremost jack breeder. (Pettis County Historical Society Collection)

This Longwood road maintenance crew had their work cut out for them in the World War I era. Graveled roads were scarce in Pettis County until after 1920 when motorists began to demand hard-surfaced roads. (Ruby K. Schondelmeyer Collection)

These men are raising the center posts for a large corn crib on the W. A. Claycomb farm about 1914. Barn building, like much else on the farm at the time, was backbreaking work. (William B. Claycomb Collection)

Threshing day on the farm always brought lots of neighbors to help. At least nineteen men were at the John R. Field farm southwest of Longwood on this day around 1920. (Pettis County Historical Society Collection)

Farmers raised a lot of wheat in Pettis County in the World War I years. This wagonload of shocked wheat is about to be threshed. Note the mountain of straw in the background on the Claycomb farm east of Hughesville at Thornleigh. (William B. Claycomb Collection)

Above: Colonel L. M. Monsees, sons and grandsons, are on their way to success. The market for mules steadily declined after World War I, as did the fame of his Limestone Valley Farm north of Smithton. (Pettis County Historical Society Collection)

Right: Some Pettis County farmers fed silage to livestock and needed silos for its storage. W. P. Raines built this silo, reportedly the tallest in the area, on his farm northeast of Longwood about 1920. It was 75' high and 16' in diameter and is still standing. (William B. Claycomb Collection)

Facing page, above: The prosperous years of the 1910s allowed many Pettis County farmers to build houses rivaling those being built in Sedalia. William A. Claycomb built this brick house in 1917 in Longwood Township. It is owned by his family. (William B. Claycomb Collection)

Facing page, below: Stone McClure of Hughesville Township built this house shortly after World War I. Frank Faulkner of Sedalia was contractor on this house as well as the Claycomb house. It is currently the residence of Mr. and Mrs. William R. Lemons. The prosperity of the 1910s was followed by two decades of fluctuating farm depression. (William B. Claycomb Collection)

Above: The Longwood Methodist Episcopal Church South, dedicated in 1919, was said by many to have been the most beautiful country church in central Missouri. Unfortunately, a dwindling membership could not support it and it was demolished in 1965. (William B. Claycomb Collection)

Left: This idyllic scene shows Miss Ada Bothwell in the foreground on Muddy Creek below Bothwell Lodge. When new Highway 65 was built in the early 1960s, the state dug a new creek channel which effectively drained and destroyed this spot. (Pettis County Historical Society Collection)

Above: These boys enjoyed playing in what may be Muddy Creek north of Sedalia and south of Thornleigh. The last of the old iron bridges on Muddy Creek was replaced in 1997. (William B. Claycomb Collection)

Facing page, below: Honorable John Bothwell started construction of his "lodge" six miles north of Sedalia in 1897 and kept working on it for thirty years. The Cliff House is on the left. Both houses are now part of the 234-acre Bothwell Lodge State Historic Site. (Ed Brummet Collection)

John H. Bothwell helped his neighbors build this attractive school five miles north of Sedalia in 1916, and it was named in his honor. It served the community for fifty years until the 105 district was absorbed by the Sedalia 200 district. The school, its teacherage (barely visible in the rear), and three acres are now in private hands. (Ed Brummet Collection)

Ringen School District No. 1 (Bothwell, No. 105, was last) was located at Lutman, about six miles south of Smithton. It closed in 1952 when the nine-square-mile district was absorbed by the Smithton district. Since then the schoolhouse has been used as a community and 4-H center and is well maintained. (Ed Brummet Collection)

Above: German Catholics had an early presence in Pettis County. They organized St. John's Catholic Church in the southeast corner of Pettis County in 1838 and later moved it three miles northwest to Bahner. A schoolhouse and cemetery join it on the west. (Ed Brummet Collection)

SEDALIA
TRUST COMPANY
Mrs COLLIE
MILLINER
T.W. ALTON
LAWYER

Chapter Five

Above: Detail of view from Fourth and Ohio Streets.

Left: Straw boaters were the fashion for men on hot summer days in the 1920s. This picture looks north from Fourth and Ohio Streets. The Sedalia Trust Company was remodeled in the late 1920s. It closed February 8, 1932. (William B. Claycomb Collection)

Above, left: Helen Gallie Steele (1862–1920) served as president of the Ladies Musical Club from 1898 to 1920. After her death the club was renamed the Helen G. Steele Music Club in her honor. Today its membership numbers over 150 ladies. The Music Club has shared the Heard Memorial Club House with Sorosis, another ladies club, since 1935. (Ed Brummet Collection)

Above, right: Beulah Harris Yancey (1874–1962) was a pillar of Sedalia's music community for most of her long life. She served as president of the Helen G. Steele Music Club from 1920 until her death in 1962 except for two years at the time of her husband's death. Her husband was Dr. Edwin F. Yancey (1858–1941), longtime chief surgeon of the Katy Railroad. (Ed Brummet Collection)

Sedalia's 1920 population was 21,144, up nearly 19 percent from that of 1910. It retained its rank of sixth largest city in the state. The new decade brought memorable social, cultural, and political change—some of it naively misguided, some of it long overdue, and some of it unwanted and seemingly beyond the control of law and economics. In 1920 the Eighteenth Amendment gave us Prohibition and the rise of organized crime; the Nineteenth Amendment provided for women's suffrage. The resurgence of the Ku Klux Klan, corruption at all levels of government, and an almost blind faith in capitalism and its benefits were all part of the scene. But it was also a time of innovation in art, literature, music, and design. More affordable products than ever before were available to consumers of all classes—perhaps none with more ramifications than the automobile. It was a decade of striking contrasts: here and there prosperity and poverty, a revival in the arts, and modest social progress undermined by corruption, lawlessness, and bigotry. Sedalia was part of this ambivalent milieu.

Charles E. Yeater (1861–1943) married Elizabeth Doyle (1880–1972) after the death of his first wife. Mr. Yeater, an attorney, was a state senator in the 1890s at the time of the capital removal scheme. He served as vice governor/acting governor of the Philippine Islands after World War I. Mrs. Yeater left the bulk of her estate to State Fair Community College to finance a library/classroom building named in memory of Governor Yeater. (Ed Brummet Collection)

Prohibition grew out of the religious revivalism of the antebellum period that eventually found political expression when the Prohibition Party was founded in 1869. Prior to 1906 the national government had left liquor control to state and local governments, but in that year the Anti-Saloon League and its supporters renewed their demand for national Prohibition.

Missouri was one of seventeen states that opted for local option. Leaving liquor control to political subdivisions insured a crazy quilt of "wet" jurisdictions where liquor could be sold, and "dry" where it could not. By 1917 eighty-five Missouri counties were dry; nineteen counties and the City of St. Louis were wet. However, there were wet cities in dry counties, dry cities in wet counties, and wet counties adjoining dry counties. Whiskey was never too far away from those who wanted it.

Sedalia was part of an area in west central Missouri that was semi-wet. The other principal wet areas were Kansas City–St. Joseph and St. Louis south along the Mississippi River to the Cape Girardeau vicinity. Most of the larger towns outside these areas were also wet. Only the Ozarks were "bone-dry."

Bowing to Anti-Saloon League pressure and using the World War I food-control bill as precedent, the federal government finally stepped in to regulate the manufacture, sale, and transportation of intoxicating beverages. On September 8, 1917, the manufacture of whiskey was prohibited in the United States. On December 18 of that year Congress proposed the

Above: Thomas W. Bast designed Smith-Cotton High School with the aid of William B. Ittner, prominent St. Louis architect famous for this school buildings. When it opened in 1926, it was arguably the finest and handsomest building between Jefferson City and Kansas City. (Ed Brummet Collection)

Top of page. left: The current Pettis County courthouse was completed in 1925 at a cost of $400,000. William E. Hulse of Hutchinson, Kansas, was the architect and his design was criticized by some because it put the more important county offices on the second floor rather than the more convenient first floor. Despite some unfortunate alterations and accretions, it remains a source of civic pride. (Ed Brummet Collection)

Top of page, right: Judge John L. McCurdy (1863–1945) is the only person to have held the offices of eastern, western, and presiding judge of the Pettis County Court. He was presiding judge in 1924 when the present courthouse was built. He married Mary Fristoe of Longwood Township and lived on a 400-acre farm in southeast Hughesville Township. (Pettis County Historical Society Collection)

Above: Smith-Cotton stands on the second highest spot (920') between St. Louis and Lee's Summit. The highest at 922' is two blocks east of Crown Hill Cemetery in extreme northeast Sedalia. (Ed Brummet Collection)

Facing page: Mrs. Sarah E. Cotton (1831–1930), daughter of George R. Smith, poses on the steps of her mansion on East Broadway. "Sedalia" is derived from her nickname, "Sed." She and her sister, Martha, gave several gifts of land to Sedalia, mostly in memory of their father. Neither of the Smith daughters left any descendants. (Ed Brummet Collection)

Thomas W. Bast (1863–1933), architect, designed all the state fair buildings up to 1926, all the Sedalia elementary schools, Smith-Cotton High School (with William B. Ittner), Convention Hall, Union Savings Bank, Bothwell Hospital, and part of Bothwell Lodge, among many other commissions. (Pettis County Historical Society Collection)

Eighteenth Amendment to the state legislatures. The U.S. secretary of state proclaimed its adoption by the required thirty-six states (three-fourths of the forty-eight states) on January 29, 1919. The manufacture of beer was prohibited May 1 and on July 1 the National Prohibition Act went into effect, outlawing the sale of all intoxicating liquor. At this time 90 percent of the land area in the country was already dry and 70 percent of the population lived in this territory. Thirty-one states were dry. To enforce the impending amendment throughout the country Congress adopted the Volstead Act October 18, 1919, over President Woodrow Wilson's veto. To the surprise of many and dismay of some, the act defined intoxicating liquor as any with as little as one-half of one percent or more of alcohol. It also made the commissioner of internal revenue of the Treasury Department responsible for enforcement of Prohibition. The Eighteenth Amendment officially became part of the Constitution on January 16, 1920, triggering enforcement of the National Prohibition Act. The Amendment prohibited the "manufacture, sale, or transportation of intoxicating liquors within, the importation thereof into, or the exportation thereof from the United States and all territory subject to the jurisdiction thereof for beverage purposes . . . " Medicinal purposes, however, were exempted.

Sedalia had one brewery, the Moerschel Brewing Company at the northwest corner of Main and Missouri Avenue. Just behind it across the Missouri Pacific tracks was the Old Missouri Distillery. The largest liquor business was that of E. G. Cassidy and Company, on Main and Moniteau Streets. Mr. Cassidy was the local distributor of Lemp's Beer, among his other enterprises. The Volstead Act, of course, closed these businesses as well as Sedalia's two dozen saloons.

Using the "medicinal" loophole, Sedalia and Pettis County doctors were soon prescribing whiskey to patients for various ailments. For instance, one of Sedalia's nine drugstores filled 349 prescriptions for whiskey and two for wine in November 1922. Eighty-eight percent were for men, twelve percent for women. Prescribed by the pint, whiskey cost $3 plus the $2 physician's fee. At $5 per pint, twice as many prescriptions were

Above: After the wheat is cut and bound into shocks, the shocks are stacked by hand to cure and dry and await the threshing machine, which will "separate the wheat from the chaff." This scene is on Cedar Creek northeast of Sedalia. John Bronson is on the left. (Rich Mewes Collection)

Top of page: Jesse Wheeler is using a "binder" to prepare his wheat for threshing. The binder cuts and binds the wheat into bundles, or shocks. (Rich Mewes Collection)

C. D. Mockbee and friends display items available at his store in Hughesville. Left to right: unidentified, R. E. Bealert, Mockbee, and Henry Martin. (Joe Henry Martin Collection)

filled from middle-class west Sedalia as from the working-class east side. Those prescribed medicinal spirits were scattered across the social and professional spectrum, ranging from poor unemployed widows, shoeshine "boys," and teamsters to bank presidents, lawyers, and bookkeepers.

And not to be forgotten, local bootleggers were doing a brisk business. Occasionally law enforcement officials arrested bootleggers, confiscated their stills and products, and prosecuted and sentenced them to jail terms. The activity of other bootleggers was overlooked.

On July 1, 1922, 1,047 Missouri Pacific and 375 MK&T shopmen walked out as part of a nationwide railroad strike. At first 350 Missouri Pacific employees, including 40 foremen, remained on the job, as did 15 Katy foremen. They, too, walked out July 10. Four hundred thousand railroad employees nationwide eventually walked out, crippling the nation's railway system. The strike was called to protest management's practice of contracting out shop labor, elimination of overtime pay for Sundays and holidays, and a proposed cut in wages.

Missouri Governor Hyde mobilized 4,021 national guard troops July 8 to meet the "insurrection" in the state. Sixty-three deputy U.S. Marshals were sent to Sedalia to keep the peace in the midst of an increasingly bitter strike. With 1,800 men on strike, an estimated one-third of Sedalia's 21,000 population was directly affected by the walk-out. Many men and families left Sedalia to look for work, boarding houses closed, and businesses downtown were hurt. Those who stayed and returned to work were deeply resented by those who did not. Families were reported to have been divided over the strike, and, in some cases, they quit speaking to one another. The personal animosity and bitterness created by the strike had neither before nor since been equaled.

After many months, management told strikers if they did not come back to work, they would never be rehired. Some returned to work; others did not. The slow decline of Sedalia as a major railroad center dates from this memorable strike.

Sedalia's economy faltered because of the strike, but by the end of the decade it seemed to have improved. Some $3.5 million was spent on capital improvements to the city, including Smith-Cotton High School constructed at a cost of $450,000; the Bothwell Hotel, $410,000; Bothwell Hospital, $215,000; four grade schools; two new bank buildings; and the Pettis County Courthouse, $400,000. Pettis Countians voted down three bond propositions after the 1920 fire, but finally passed a $350,000 bond

Early road graders like the one on the right were pulled by steam engine. This one, parked behind the Bealert Store in Hughesville, was used on the community's mostly dirt roads. The Bank of Hughesville can be seen to the left of the two-story building. (Joe Henry Martin Collection)

There were apparently no laws in the 1920s requiring gasoline pumps to be at least a few yards from buildings. Note the pump is hand-operated. The Hughesville businessman is Roll Bealert. (Joe Henry Martin Collection)

issue in 1923. The $50,000 insurance proceeds made up the difference. The handsome three-story courthouse measures 136 feet long, 96 feet wide, and 55 feet high. It was dedicated in May 1925, and remains a source of civic pride.

There were ominous overtones in 1926 of things to come. On June 16 the Farmers and Mechanics Bank closed. Two days later, the American Exchange Bank across the street also closed. Both banks went into liquidation under the same receiver, T. H. Yount of Sedalia, who combined the liquidation operations of the relatively small banks. These bankruptcies seem not to have caused great concern; four banks remained. Out in the county, the Bank of Hughesville had closed in 1925, and the other county banks were losing deposits as a result of a farm depression that dated from 1920. The high grain and livestock prices of the World War I period broke in 1920 and, together with land, suffered an erratic decline throughout the decade. Bankers began to foreclose on mortgages secured by farmland worth less than half its 1920 value. Those carefully reading the periodically published statements of condition of the Sedalia banks were watching their deposits decline as well. But more seriously, cash and high-quality assets easily converted to cash, such as government bonds, were drying up while loans, especially farm loans, remained stable and in some cases actually increased. The reader would have also noticed increasing amounts payable by local banks to city banks.

It was also in 1926 that a gang of young bootleggers and bank robbers spectacularly self-destructed. Led by, of all people, a smart and charismatic thirty-seven-year-old criminal defense lawyer named Claude Wilkerson, the gang of young men and assorted girlfriends had been busily sticking up small area banks and dealing in bootleg whiskey for several years. Wilkerson's most famous and revealing statement was in response to a

Mrs. Charles Beatty was the wife of the depot agent at Hughesville. The Missouri Pacific got permission to abandon the old Lexington Branch between Sedalia and Lexington in the mid-1960s, and the depot was demolished. The water tank is barely visible on the right. (Joe Henry Martin Collection)

man who asked him how much it would cost to get his son off a burglary charge. "Three hundred dollars," Wilkerson supposedly replied; "$100 for the cops, $100 for the prosecuting attorney, and $100 for me." Self-serving and perhaps a lie, yet no one seems to have questioned the "fee." Two of the young men were ambushed and killed under mysterious circumstances September 11, 1926, in the middle of Flat Creek at the Grand Avenue Ford. They had been scheduled to testify in Boonville on bank robbery charges against Wilkerson. On December 27, Wilkerson himself was shot and killed downtown by the father of one of the boys killed in September. The rest of the gang were taken into custody or disappeared. The father was acquitted of murder by reason of self-defense in 1927, notwithstanding his ambush of Wilkerson.

Above: This was the first engine turned out of the Sedalia Missouri Pacific Shops under the production system inaugurated after the great 1922 strike. This May 1925, picture shows supervisors lined up beside Engine Number 1223. (Pettis County Historical Society Collection)

Left: The Masonic Lodge's "Karem Kararan" car was a special assignment for the Katy Shops paint crew. (Ed Brummet Collection)

The Katy Shops paint crew posed for this picture in the 1920s. Foreman Rowlette is in bowler hat at far left. (Ed Brummet Collection)

In 1928 there was a movement in the townships to build gravel-surface connecting roads to the newly built federal highways and Sedalia's Twelve Mile Road District, with gravel roads already extending six miles in all directions from Sedalia. Heath's Creek Township's Road District, soon joined by Longwood's, led the way by voting in favor of a $25,000 bond issue to be matched by the County Court. Heath's Creek–Longwood was soon joined by the Hughesville and, then, Houstonia Road Districts. The latter passed a $54,000 bond on June 23, 1928. In September 1928, the small Thornleigh District in southern Longwood Township unanimously passed a $10,000 bond to be matched by the County Court. The LaMonte District was planning a $75,000 bond issue by fall. In the span of one year, some 150 miles of gravel roads costing $600,000 were agreed upon, financed, and put under construction to be completed by 1930. Considering the farm community's increasing distress, this was a noteworthy achievement and speaks well of the commissioners' leadership. (Each district had a three-commissioner board.) Responsibility for this system of roads, soon to be called "farm-to-market," was assumed by the state in the 1930s. The farm-to-market roads were finally "blacktopped" in the 1950s.

In the fall of 1931 the Crawford Loan and Abstract Company, a private loan company at 410 South Ohio, Sedalia, holding mortgages on hundreds of Pettis County farms, went into bankruptcy. Its president, Grant Crawford, had been vice president of the $3,000,000 Citizens National Bank since 1909, as

Above, left & right: This automobile was decorated for a 1924 Katy Railroad promotional parade. (Ed Brummet Collection)

well as a large borrower. He had been making and then selling farm real estate loans for thirty years to local and Eastern investors. Most of his loans were now in default.

Late Sunday afternoon, November 1, William H. Powell, Crawford's friend and president of the Citizens National Bank, shot himself. His bank at the southeast corner of Main and Ohio Streets, the largest in the area, closed the next day. Powell died the following Wednesday. On January 28, 1932, Charles C. Evans of the Sedalia Trust Company, shot and killed himself. His $600,000 company closed February 8. On February 15 Conrad H. Bothwell, president of the Sedalia National Bank with assets of $1,000,000, seems to have panicked and closed his bank. The panic was contagious despite the efforts of local officials and newspapers to dampen it.

Meanwhile, banks outside Sedalia in the county were closing—the LaMonte Bank on September 14, 1931; the Bank of Longwood on November 3; and the People's Bank of Green Ridge on January 20, 1932. Six Pettis County banks with assets of $4,562,000 closed in a five-month period. All went into receiverships and liquidations lasting up to five years. In 1926 there had been seven banks in Sedalia; by February 1932, only the Third National Bank and tiny Union Savings Bank remained, although later in that year investors led by John McGrath (son-in-law of E. G. Cassidy) organized the Sedalia Bank and Trust Company. These banks survived the depression and prospered in the postwar years.

The events of the winter of 1931–1932 had a devastating impact on most Pettis Countians. For instance, the Citizens National Bank's six thousand depositors lost fifty-one cents on the dollar, and even the forty-nine cents they recovered took many years to receive. The stockholders in the bankrupt banks, of course, lost all their investments. The hundreds of investors in Crawford Loan and Abstract Company real estate notes also lost hundreds of thousands of dollars. Its receiver, Donnohue Loan and

Investment Company, foreclosed on hundreds of Pettis County farms and managed them for decades until they were finally sold. In the darkest days of the depression there simply was little if any money to be had. Franklin Roosevelt's New Deal pumped several million dollars into the county which alleviated distress somewhat. The aid and welfare programs ranged from the sprawling Osage Cooperative Farm in north Pettis County to WPA road, bridge, and school projects; and from U.S. Department of Agriculture "Triple A" farm subsidy payments to a mattress factory, to name but a few.

Because supply far exceeded demand, prices were low and those people with safe and steady jobs managed the depression relatively well. Some were even able to buy deeply discounted notes on Pettis County farms, and watch those farms steadily rise in value after World War II. But such opportunity was not common. The majority of the people were living all but "hand-to-mouth." They survived the depression, too, but some were embittered by their losses and hardships and felt betrayed by their bankers and "the system." The system changed and New Deal innovations such as the Federal Deposit Insurance Corporation and Rural Electrification Administration restored most people's confidence in banks and capitalism in general, although it took World War II to actually pull Sedalia, Pettis County, and the country out of the Great Depression. Life in Pettis County was never the same after the winter of 1931–1932. A generation's fear and disillusionment abated in time, but its caution did not.

Global insecurities began to mingle with domestic insecurities, and then to gradually overwhelm them as war resumed in Europe in

Sedalia's old First Baptist Church was built in 1924 at the southeast corner of Sixth and Lamine. The church was founded in 1865 and today occupies this entire block. This building was replaced in 1976 with a new sanctuary at Seventh and Lamine. (Sedalia Public Library Collection)

The handsome Bothwell Hotel opened in 1927. John H. Bothwell felt Sedalia needed a first-class hotel and he invested $50,000 to help build one. His investment was bequeathed to the city when he died in 1929. This picture dates from the late 1940s. (Sedalia Public Library Collection)

September 1939. While the United States did not exactly remain neutral early in the war, it did stay out of it over two years until December 7, 1941. Subsequent to Pearl Harbor the United States found itself in the midst of a world at war. Before it was finally over four long years later, approximately 3,120 Pettis County men and women either volunteered or were drafted into the armed services. This was about 19 percent of the male population, only slightly higher than in World War I. The number of women in uniform, however, was significantly higher this time. One hundred thirty eight lost their lives, 4.4 percent of those who served. An untold number were injured.

Once again Pettis Countians were being exhorted to buy war bonds. For example, the county's quota for the first quarter of 1943 was $300,000. It was exceeded by $14,943.50 and a bomber was named for the county. The Treasury raised the county's quota for the second quarter 63 percent to $488,000, and when sales lagged the local newspaper implied that the county was shirking its patriotic duty.

There were other quotas to meet. Pettis County's scrap metal quota was 1,750 tons, or 100 pounds per person. There were five rationing boards: fuel, commodities, food, tire, and gas mileage. On December 1, 1942,

Sedalia was put under rent control, retroactive to March 1 levels. The boards were under the supervision of the Pettis County Council of Civilian Defense, also responsible for blackout drills designed to make Sedalia invisible in case of nighttime air raid. Air raid wardens were charged with enforcing blackouts. The War Production Board banned all outside Christmas decorations in 1942. School children were enlisted to collect fat and flax, as well as scrap iron and other commodities, for the war effort. The Pettis County War Board's principal responsibility was to encourage farmers to increase food production with less farm manpower. All the county's farm agencies were represented on the War Board, chaired by the county's Agricultural Adjustment Administration's chairman. Men exempt from the draft and women, mostly single, left the state for relatively good paying jobs in the defense industry or federal government. Dislocations were part of many people's lives, civilians as well as military.

With the war over in Europe, GIs were shipped home on furlough before they were to be shipped out again to join their comrades in the western Pacific for the scheduled fall 1945 invasion of Japan. Two atomic bombs in August made the invasion unnecessary, and while their use was controversial, none of the exhausted GIs second-guessed President Harry Truman's decision to drop the bombs.

For most of five years normal life had been put on hold—families, children, houses, cars, and public projects. Now that Germany, central Europe, and Japan lay in ruin, the returning GIs wanted something more than "normalcy." A grateful Congress gave them a "GI Bill" that would, in half a generation, put many of them firmly in the middle class and pave the way for the postwar consumer society. They also began fathering what would come to be known as the Baby Boomers.

This 1930 post office at Fourth and Lamine replaced the old 1892 post office at Second and Lamine. It was replaced in 1968 by the current post office on East Fifth Street. It now houses the local Social Security office. (Sedalia Public Library Collection)

Above: The Katy's Coach Shop Band performs at the grandstand at the Missouri State Fair circa 1930. Otto Meyer, behind the base drum, is director. J. Harry Brunckhorst, Katy shop superintendent, is front row left and Wayne Mountjoy is second from right in third row. (Rosalie Knight Collection)

Facing page, above: Firemen pose in 1930 with their Monarch pumper at Station No. 2. They are Chief W. H. Paul, Foreman John Lueck, Fred Brummet, Ora Martin, Bill Collins, and Bill Middleton. The mascot is not identified. (Ed Brummet Collection)

Facing page, below: Arator School (No. 10) was located less than three miles north of Smithton near Limestone Valley Farm. Gladys Ferguson (1903–1963), who taught there from 1925–1939, is remembered for the many blue ribbons the school exhibits won at the Missouri State Fair under her guidance. This picture of her and her forty-some students dates from the early 1930's. (Pettis County Historical Society Collection)

SEDALIA

KDRO
BROADCASTING STUDIO
OFFICES

Above: Okee and Iva Rice owned and operated the world's largest White Leghorn chicken hatchery until the mid-1940s. Started at Green Ridge, hatcheries were later built on Highway 65 south of Sedalia. A few buildings remain, although long ago converted for other uses. (Sedalia Public Library Collection)

Facing page, above, left: KDRO, Sedalia's first radio station, went on the air in 1939. In the 1960s this building at West Broadway and State Fair Boulevard was enlarged to accommodate KMOS-TV, and later demolished. It is now the site of a Mercantile Bank facility. (Sedalia Public Library Collection)

Facing page, above right: Professor C. C. Hubbard (circa 1875–1947) was born in Glasgow, Missouri. He was graduated from Lincoln University in 1896, and, after serving as principal in Tipton and Paris schools, came to Sedalia in 1906 where he served as principal of Lincoln School until his death on May 23, 1947. A new high school for blacks was built in 1927 and named for Professor Hubbard in 1943, as was a park. Under his leadership, both Lincoln and Hubbard Schools were fully accredited and attracted many students from surrounding counties. A no-nonsense educator from the "old school," he demanded the best of his students and teachers, and got it. Integration eventually closed Hubbard and the adjoining Lincoln Elementary School in the early 1960s. (Ed Brummet Collection)

Facing page, below: The National Guard Armory, built in 1938 by the WPA, was home to Battery C 1st Howitzer Battalion 128th Artillery and Headquarters 135th Artillery Group. It is still headquarters of the 135th Artillery Brigade. (Sedalia Public Library Collection)

These beautiful roller bearing steam engines were reportedly constructed at the Missouri Pacific shops in the 1930s. They are said to have "rolled up splendid mileage during the war (WWII) years." (Pettis County Historical Society Collection)

MISSOURI PACIFIC
5305
5305

MISSOURI PACIFIC LINES
5324
5324

Above: This speaker (left center) has attracted a large crowd to the Highway Gardens at the state fair. Most of the ladies and many of the men wore hats in these days just prior to World War II. (Sedalia Public Library Collection)

Top of page: The boys on parade west of the grandstand have drawn a large state fair crowd. Another group of uniformed boys appear to be waiting their turn in the right background. (Sedalia Public Library Collection)

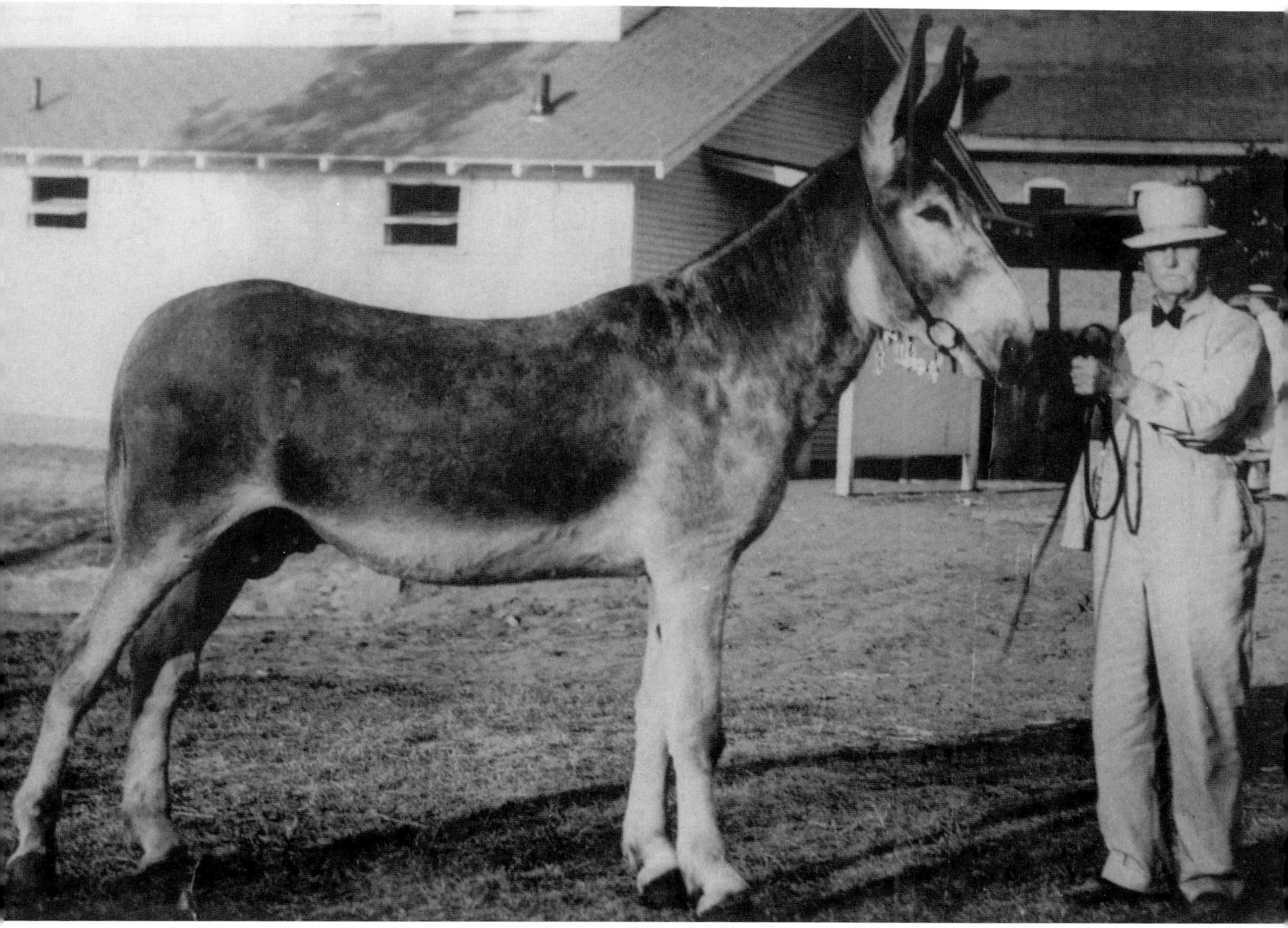

Colonel L. M. Monsees exhibits a prize jack at the Missouri State Fair shortly before his death in 1947. Mr. Monsees lost his right arm in a shooting accident at age thirty-eight. (Pettis County Historical Society Collection)

The Sedalia Police Department and other officials gathered for this group picture circa 1940. Longtime Highway Patrol Officer Pete Stohr is on the rear row extreme right. Chief Anson Finnell is between the two civilians in the front row. (Pettis County Historical Society Collection)

Chief Anson Finnell poses in front of the old City Hall during World War II. In those days many downtown street corners had service stations, such as the Texaco station on the southeast corner of Second and Osage Streets in the background. (Pettis County Historical Society Collection)

Above: The roster of the first Sedalia Merchants team (1945) included: first row left to right, Joe Wolford, Juicey Spriggs, Don Richardson, Gus Shirley, Millard Humes, "Bus" Livengood, Emery Ellsworth; back row left to right, Wilber Rothganger, Palmer Nichols, John Thomas, Edward Christian, Raymond Morris, Harold Green. Bat boy, Bud Thomas. The Sedalia Athletics and Sedalia Blues were earlier teams. (Pettis County Historical Society Collection)

Left: This 1942 handbill needs no explanation. The West Second Street address was only a few yards east of the police station and was the scene of a murder when a game went awry in 1947. (Sedalia Public Library Collection)

Facing page: Betty Ruth Ream, daughter of Mr. and Mrs. Thomas J. Ream of Hughesville, was Miss Missouri in 1945. Here she is shown on the boardwalk at Atlantic City. Miss Ream, a graduate of Hughesville High School and Central College, is the only Pettis Countian to be "Miss Missouri." (Betty Finley Collection)

Presenting
Miss Missouri

Chapter Six

The Chamber of Commerce sponsored quarterly courtesy awards around 1950. Swafford's Service Station at 323 South Osage was a winner in the days of full service. The Swafford Service Station corner later became the location of Farm and Home Savings and Loan, then Roosevelt Bank, and finally a Mercantile Bank facility in 1997. (Sedalia Public Library Collection)

World War II restrictions prevented new industrial developments, but once the war was over resources were once again available for construction. The Pittsburgh Corning Corporation started construction of its new glass plant on West Sixteenth Street in 1946. (Sedalia Public Library Collection)

In 1946 the Iron Curtain was falling across Central Europe. Millions on both sides were displaced and starving. The British, French, American, and Red Armies were settling into their occupations of conquered Germany and, in Nuremberg, were trying high-ranking Nazi officials for war crimes. Japan, having suffered President Truman's "rain of ruin," lay in ashes under the able administration of General Douglas MacArthur. At home the public was demanding demobilization as soon as possible. But the world had changed, and the United States' role in the new order did not allow it to abandon its new global responsibilities. Those responsibilities came mostly by default; there was no other country able to step into postwar power vacuums except the Soviet Union, which was exploiting all opportunities that came its way, and creating them when they did not. The world stage was set for a generation of cold war in which Communist aggression would be contested and contained by the West, led by the United States.

At home, labor demands had been put on hold for the duration of the war, but now that wartime restrictions were off, the unions resumed their quarrels with management. Truman found himself dealing with restless unions threatening to strike. When railroad workers did walk off the job in Sedalia and elsewhere, the President made a threat himself to meet what he perceived to be a danger to the national interest. The strikers, quite in

Above, left: Charles Van Dyne, president of the Sedalia Chamber of Commerce, breaks ground for the Sedco Shoe Factory on North Missouri and Missouri Pacific tracks circa 1942. George Trader is fourth from right. (Sedalia Public Library Collection)

Above, right: In 1944 Town and Country Shoes moved into the Sedco Shoe Factory and remained for some forty years, reaching peak employment of about 500 in 1965. William Mathieson was the company's local manager for many years. (Sedalia Public Library Collection)

Top of page: The Pittsburgh Corning glass plant started production in 1947 and has been an industrial mainstay since then. The farmland behind the plant is now filled with residential and commercial development on and near Thompson Boulevard. (Sedalia Public Library Collection)

Above, left: Sedalia gave the Missouri Pacific Railroad $200,000 cash and 125 acres in east Sedalia valued at $25,000 to secure the shops in 1904. The massive facility employed up to 1,400 men in its heyday, but is now almost empty. The vacant yards are for sale. (Ed Brummet Collection)

Above, right: Bob Overstreet, right, presents Mr. and Mrs. Marvin Goodwin with a $25 War Bond. The bond was the Balanced Farming Program's first prize and was presented at the Soils and Crops Conference at Convention Hall on January 13, 1948. (Sedalia Public Library Collection)

violation of their Constitutional rights, would be drafted into the military if they did not return to work. The union backed down and the nation's railroads resumed operations.

Meanwhile in Pettis County the veterans were filtering home, the vast majority easily making the transition to civilian life and not overly concerned with European politics. There was a housing shortage in Sedalia. The demand for houses was met with new rental units built in people's backyards; prefabricated, somewhat temporary housing in new subdivisions; and blocks of new "ranch-style" houses, mostly in west Sedalia.

In the county, the Central Missouri Rural Electrical Cooperative resumed construction of power lines interrupted by the war. In 1940, 385 miles of line had been built in Pettis and Saline Counties, serving 1,203 farms. In 1948, there were 682 additional miles in the system and 1,873 more farms. The pace of school consolidation quickened. One-by-one the old neighborhood school districts disappeared into the consolidated districts: Hughesville, Houstonia, LaMonte, Green Ridge, Dresden, Smithton, and Sedalia, although a handful, such as Bothwell, managed to maintain their identities into the 1960s. Hughesville and Houstonia merged in 1964–1965 to create Northwest R5. Pettis County lost several districts in the south and southwest to Cole Camp and Windsor and R1 in the northwest corner to Sweet Springs. By the early 1950s the consolidated districts were building additions to their school facilities to meet the first wave of Baby Boomers. The Sedalia 200 District also went on an extensive building program that included gymnasiums and cafeterias as well as classrooms. All of these capital improvements were financed by general obligation bonds.

In 1950 North Korea invaded South Korea. The administration perceived the North to be a proxy of and the invasion provocation by Communist China and/or the Soviet Union, and decided to make a stand. General MacArthur, under the technical auspices of the United Nations, was ordered to organize the defense of South Korea. With the Korean War, never declared, came war bond, renamed Defense Bonds, quotas once again. Pettis Countians purchased $817,063 in 1951. The same year Congress appropriated $22,462,000 to reactivate the old Sedalia Army Air Field at Knob Noster. Seventeen Pettis Countians were killed in Korea before President Dwight Eisenhower accepted a status quo truce shortly after taking office in 1953. The new administration increased the Sedalia Air Field appropriation to $26,500,000, and renamed it Whiteman Air Force Base on December 3, 1955,

The world premiere of the B-movie Scudda Hoo! Scudda Hay! *was held at the Fox Theater March 10, 1948. Here the stars clown with a mule in front of the theater. The heavy snowfall that day did not prevent smiles all around. (Sedalia Public Library Collection)*

in honor of pilot Lieutenant George Whiteman of Sedalia, killed at Pearl Harbor.

By this time the Soviet Union also had the Bomb and the Cold War arms race was on. Throughout the 1950s the United States routinely and recklessly, if unintentionally, conducted atomic and later hydrogen bomb tests in the Nevadan desert that, we now know, unevenly contaminated Pettis County and all the country east of California with radioactive fallout. By the end of the decade, public and private bomb shelters were naively promoted in the popular press as protection against nuclear attack. As it turned out, the only radiation we were exposed to was our own.

On a more constructive note, the Eisenhower administration launched the Interstate Highway System, selling it as a defense system doubling as a network of superhighways that would easily and quickly move men and material around the country if military necessity dictated it. Few probably believed that in 1955, and fewer still would have predicted the economic and social impact the system, built over thirty-five years, would have on the nation. Not, however, directly on Pettis County—I-70 missed it by two miles. The decade's quintessential year may be 1958. The following table shows how some Sedalia businesses and professions have changed, or not, with the times.

	1958	1998
Population	20,354	19,800
Bank Locations	3	16
Savings and Loans	2	0
Barbers	20	6
Churches	50	51
Gasoline Stations	40	17
Grocery Stores	45	8
Lawyers	19	38
Liquor Stores	6	6
Taverns	19	6
Physicians, MDs and DOs	33	39
Restaurants—total	43	50
Chain-owned Restaurants	0	22

Cars of 1958 sported pounds of chrome and ever-rising tail fins. Elvis Presley had already created a new popular music; Dr. Jonas Salk had developed his polio vaccine. The nation was at peace, proud of its military power, and increasingly prosperous in its private and public sectors. Sedalia built football and Little League stadiums for its Baby Boomers and a $600,000 addition to the Bothwell Hospital, complete with an innovative

Above, left: After the Rice Leghorn Hatchery closed, Iva Rice opened her famous restaurant, the Old Missouri Homestead, in the old YMCA Building. The popular "Garden" was located in the basement. The restaurant burned in 1986. (Sedalia Public Library Collection)

Above, right: The demand for postwar housing in Sedalia was partly met with prefabricated houses manufactured by Home Building Corporation at 303 North Park, Sedalia. This house is typical of the kind sold to returning veterans. (Sedalia Public Library Collection)

Crippled Children's Center. Its public school system, under the longtime able leadership of Dr. Heber Hunt, remained among the best in the state; and tree-lined Broadway was still the most handsome boulevard in central Missouri. But Sedalia had long ago lost its rank as sixth largest town in the state, not so much because it was losing population—it was not—but because it had been left behind by more aggressive or rapidly growing suburban towns. There were few glamorous public projects, and downtown Sedalia was more or less doing business as it had for decades, not to mention looking the same. When it shortly began to "modernize" its "look," much of the town's architectural heritage was either demolished for parking lots or hidden behind aluminum fronts. Worse, too long overly dependent on the railroads, the town's industrial base still lacked widespread diversity. However, the city was about to get a big, if temporary, boost from an unexpected quarter, due to no initiative of its own.

Sedalia celebrated its centennial in 1960 and the next year the Air Force announced that Whiteman Air Force Base, which had been a Strategic Air Command (SAC) base in the 1950s, would henceforth be the home of its 351st Intercontinental Ballistic Missile Wing. The Air Force proposed to build one hundred fifty "launch facilities" and fifteen "launch control facilities" for Minuteman nuclear missiles to be scattered over fifty-three hundred square miles and fourteen counties in west central Missouri. The Air Force did not ask anyone's opinion on the massive project, and surprisingly the public asked few if any questions about it. Any vague apprehensions the public may have had were overwhelmed by the prospect of job opportunities and the millions of dollars to be pumped

Above: Governor Forrest Smith, center, visits the Missouri State Fair circa 1949. (Sedalia Public Library Collection)

Right: An unidentified man gives Governor Forrest Smith a champion country cured ham at the annual state fair ham breakfast around 1951. The ham breakfast is still a popular event. Note the governor's colorful state fair tie. (Sedalia Public Library Collection)

Facing page: George E. Chamberlin operated Chamberlin's Service Station at 2600 West Broadway for many years. (Ed Brummet Collection)

into the local economy. Some 10 percent of the missiles were planted in Pettis County and the entire system, connected by 1,777 miles of buried cable, was activated in 1966. The missiles, later upgraded to Minuteman II status, were 57.6 feet long, 6 feet in diameter, and weighed 36 tons—all presumably locked on targets in the Soviet Union. Pettis County, of course, was now a prime target for Soviet missiles, but Sedalia overlooked that distinction and welcomed the population increase and the tens of millions of dollars spent in town. Until, four years later, the construction was completed and the boomlet collapsed when Boeing and its subcontractors moved on to other projects. Thirty years later, pursuant to the START agreements, the system was deactivated and dismantled while Whiteman became the home of B-2 Stealth Bombers, carrying more firepower than the old Minuteman IIs.

By 1966 young men's draft boards had become a big part of their lives. The Selective Service had the job of filling the ranks for a growing war in Southeast Asia where field commanders' troop demands were ever higher, as were the local monthly draft quotas, running between two and three dozen. If one lost his deferment and passed his physical, the Pettis County Draft Board had him in uniform in less than three months. All but a handful

The old 1890s James Glass mansion at Seventh and Osage Streets became the Ewing Funeral Home in 1935. The home's ambulance and hearse are proudly displayed in this 1949 photograph. The funeral homes provided ambulance service to the community for decades. (Sedalia Public Library Collection)

eventually got orders for Vietnam where most spent twelve anxious months. Twelve Pettis County men lost their lives in a misguided and seemingly endless war that was a catalyst for profound social, cultural, and political change at home. The older Baby Boomers fought the war as well as dodged it and/or protested it by march and riot and the public burning of draft cards. But the war ground on until American guns were turned on American students with lethal effect, and the befuddled public support for the war ebbed away.

By the mid-1960s, just as the Minuteman boomlet died, a handful of Sedalians recognized the complacency responsible for the eroding industrial base and determined to do something about it. Realizing that good paying jobs would have to be pursued, the town took its first tentative steps toward organized industrial development.

It was suggested that "a facility for higher education and training" was needed to attract industry and the hoped-for jobs. The Sedalia Jaycees agreed to lead the effort to establish a community college district in Pettis and Benton Counties. There was support for the district in Pettis County,

Above: The Liberty Park swimming pool was one of the several public recreational facilities built in Sedalia after World War II. Built in 1949, it was demolished in 1996 and replaced with a new pool in 1997. (Sedalia Public Library Collection)

Top of page, left: The Hubbard Park swimming pool, a product of segregation, was for use by blacks. Like the Liberty Park pool, it was built in 1949. The city closed it in 1982 and later demolished it. The City Hospital No. 2 for blacks can be glimpsed in the background. It was demolished in 1997. (Sedalia Public Library Collection)

Top of page, right: The Jennie Jaynes Lewis Stadium on South Limit cost $100,000 and has a seating capacity of 3,000. Located almost two miles west of the high school it serves, it was one of the larger projects built for Baby Boomer athletes. (Sedalia Public Library Collection)

Everett Stumpf, a longtime employee of Hoffman Hardware, was the Courtesy Award winner for the first quarter 1950. Left to right: Harry Naugel, Stumpf, Arthur Hoffman, and Philip Hoffman. The award was $5. (Sedalia Public Library Collection)

but there was less interest for one in Benton County. Nonetheless, the State Board of Education approved a Pettis-Benton County junior college district in 1965, and the voters approved it in 1966. But litigation ensued and delayed meaningful action for a year or more. However, in May 1968, the district purchased 15 acres west of the State Fair grounds and took a five-year option on an additional 114 acres. State Fair Community College opened in a temporary plywood building with 404 students and eighteen instructors in September. Part of Cooper County was later added to the district and thirty years later the college has an enrollment of some 2,200 students and sixty full-time faculty members. It also has a growing campus where the half-dozen permanent buildings have been financed by benefactors, not taxpayers. While Sedalia's industrial development program has been generally successful, there have been missteps. State Fair Community College, however, under longtime capable leadership, has admirably fulfilled its mission.

The 1970s are remembered as a time of bad taste in hairstyles, clothes, interior design, and architecture; of political scandal and disgrace at the highest level; of gasoline shortages; "go-go" banking and disco music; ever-rising interest rates; and humiliations abroad. President Jimmy Carter put his finger on the spirit of the times with one word: *malaise*.

Locally, the city's industrial development efforts were beginning to pay off. Several major companies were enticed to town and brought with them jobs coveted by every small city in the Midwest. There were improvements in the city's infrastructure, and commercial development continued on the highways in southwest Sedalia while downtown became less viable. The population did not significantly change, except for one hot weekend in 1974 when an estimated 130,000 young people converged on the fair grounds for the infamous Ozark Music Festival. The year 1979 was an ambivalent one. On August 3 the Missouri secretary of state filed suit against the $6.4 million Industrial Loan and Investment Company of Sedalia, charging it with various violations of the Missouri Uniform Securities Act. It went into liquidation in December 1979. Also in August Alcolac, one of the much touted new industries and a manufacturer of chemicals in northeast Sedalia, began to blanket the countryside with "soap bubbles," an ominous harbinger of serious problems to come. Gasoline prices reached all-time high levels as OPEC increased the price of crude oil by a third. Inflation rippled through the economy and interest rates and precious metals climbed to unheard-of levels. Amidst all of this excitement, Bothwell Lodge State Park opened to the public on the fiftieth anniversary of John H. Bothwell's death. This county crown jewel came only after four years of grass-roots hard work.

In spring, 1980, Sedalia suffered its second major tornado in three years, although as in 1977, there were no deaths despite the widespread property damage. By the end of June temperatures were well above normal. In July the daytime temperatures hovered between 100° and 105° all month. The heat wave finally broke in August, but not before breaking a few farmers already suffering from record high interest rates and land prices. Determined to squeeze inflation out of the economy, the Reagan administration tightened interest rates until the prime rate reached 20 percent. Like the drought, inflation broke, but not before bankrupting

The MFA grain elevator on Clinton Road was built in the early 1950s. (Sedalia Public Library Collection)

many small businessmen. In Pettis County, farmland that sold for $1,400 per acre in 1980 sold for 40 percent of that five or six years later. Bank regulators forced country banks to transfer large sums to their reserves for bad debts to cover the farm losses, and they eventually closed twenty-nine insolvent banks in Missouri, although none in Pettis County (other than Industrial Loan in 1979, technically not a bank).

In 1981 Town and Country Shoes, with 315 employees, filed for bankruptcy and Swift and Company, with 200 employees, closed May 18, at least in part due to a dispute with the city over its $6,000-a-month sewer bill. But these job losses were offset by new industries gradually filling the city's industrial parks. Some commercial development continued on the south and west highways, but most of the residential development was outside the city limits in subdivisions like Walnut Hills and on small

Governor's Day at the Missouri State Fair was and is a time for country cured ham and politics. Left to right: Mayor Julian Bagby (partially cut out), unidentified officer, Governor Phil M. Donnelly, and Lieutenant Governor, later governor, James T. Blair, Jr., mid-1950s. (Sedalia Public Library Collection)

These groomed Herefords are being shown off outside the Coliseum. The men's coats however, suggest it was not State Fair time. The late Jack Cunningham is center rear. (Sedalia Public Library Collection)

acreages within five miles of Sedalia. Notwithstanding this modest progress, Sedalia's population declined 5.4 percent in the 1990 census. The county's population, 35,437, remained about what it had been for decades, ranking twenty-first among the state's 114 counties.

By 1997 farmland values exceeded the highs of the early 1980s, although grain prices were no better. Reflecting the national trend, fewer farmers were farming more land. Cattle feeding, once so important to Pettis County, had virtually disappeared. No longer did every farmer feed a few hogs. Only a handful did. Cow and calf herds, although not yet uncommon, were dwindling. New chicken-feeding complexes, however, dotted the rural landscape, supplying poultry to Tyson Foods' massive 1,100-acre processing plant at Dresden. Construction of confined animal-feeding operations has so far stopped at chickens, although several investors made tentative and controversial confined hog-feeding propositions in 1995. Despite the organized opposition to hog confinement facilities because of environmental concerns, the county turned down a planning and zoning proposal as it faced the twenty-first century.

••••••

When I was in the real estate business in my thirties I found myself one cold winter day in the dark, cramped home of an elderly lady. She was bedfast and I had come to get her signature on a contract. The home, an apartment, was filled with people, all of whom seemed suspicious of me. The circumstances of the contract and my attire were such that they may have thought I was a lawyer from Chicago, someone in a suit from out-of-town come to take advantage of an old lady. A man said matter-of-factly, "My cord was cut in Pettis County." For a moment I had no idea what he meant, and it made me more uneasy about a situation in which I was so outnumbered. And then I realized he meant he had been born in Pettis County, that was where his umbilical cord had been cut. It was his way of letting me know he was a native son and I was on his turf. I do not remember exactly what I said, but I let him understand that I, too, was a Pettis Countian and proud of it. There was a little laughter, the tension was broken, and the old lady signed the contract.

I thought about the incident later. The man and I had entirely different backgrounds with nothing in common except our place of birth. But when we realized we had that in common, for a minute our differences were unimportant. We called the same place home.

Above: Sedalia businessmen and public and parochial teachers met in a local theater in the early 1950s. How many can you identify? (Sedalia Public Library Collection)

Left: The Chamber of Commerce sponsored an annual 4-H Club Achievement Banquet in the 1950s. In return, Pettis County 4-H club members, parents, and leaders entertained the Chamber of Commerce and civic leaders at a Liberty Park picnic such as the one pictured here circa 1955. (Sedalia Public Library Collection)

Facing page: This float in a 1950s parade in the 200 block of West Third Street promotes Sedalia's religious, educational, recreational, industrial, and agricultural advantages. (Sedalia Public Library Collection)

The Sixth Armored Band had just passed the courthouse in this early 1950s parade. (Sedalia Public Library Collection)

Above: The Missouri Pacific Women's Club had a booth on Ohio Street at a 1950s street fair. (Sedalia Public Library Collection)

Left: Consumer products were available as never before in Sedalia stores in the 1950s. These are some of the products available, excluding the baby. (Sedalia Public Library Collection)

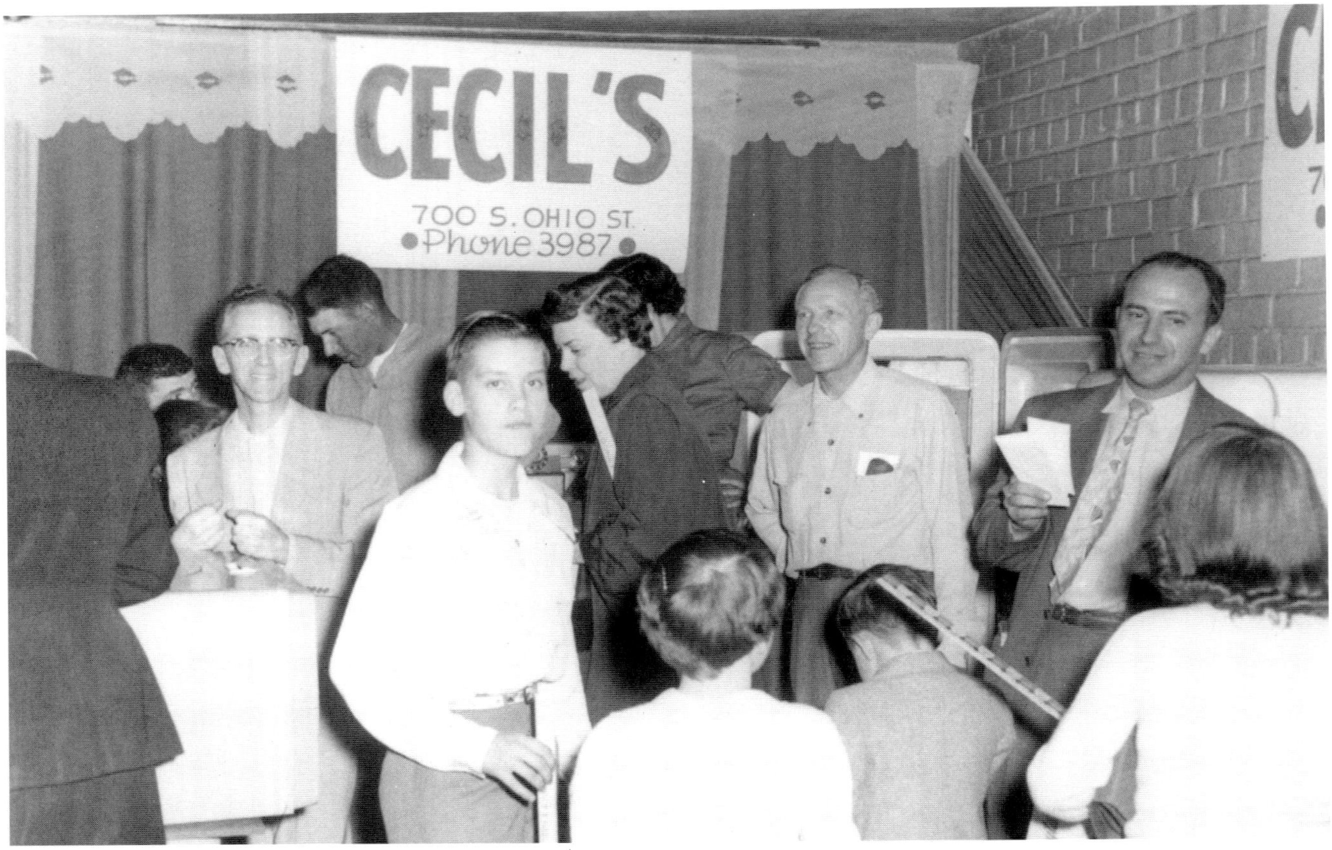

Above, left & right: The first annual Chamber of Commerce—Sedalia Air Force Base picnic was held at Liberty Park June 22, 1954. After dinner, the crowd was entertained at the old bandstand, demolished many years ago. (Sedalia Public Library Collection)

Top of page: Three of the Cecil brothers were busy greeting customers on this day in the mid-1950s. They are, left to right, Elver, Cleo, and Gerald. The boy in front is not identified. Gerald Cecil still operates the store at 700 South Ohio. (Sedalia Public Library Collection)

Above: The Sedalia Army Air Field 18 miles west of town was built as a glider training base in World War II. Sedalia made an effort in the early 1950s to locate the Air Force Academy here. When that failed, the Air Force renamed it Whiteman Air Force Base in 1955 and made it a Strategic Air Command base for a decade until the bombers were replaced in 1965 with 150 Minuteman missiles, which were themselves replaced with B-2 bombers in the 1990s. This picture was taken circa 1955. (Sedalia Public Library Collection)

Above: Throughout the 1950s the Chamber of Commerce sponsored a "Yard of the Month" contest. The Allen Duff yard at 911 West Broadway was the winner this particular month. (Sedalia Public Library Collection)

Above: The C. W. Flower Company was celebrating its fiftieth anniversary in 1954. Two years later the store expanded onto the second floor of the Katy Building at 219 South Ohio and installed the first escalator in Central Missouri. All sales transactions were sent by pneumatic tubes to bookkeeping on the mezzanine in rear. The store closed in 1989. (Ed Brummet Collection)

Left: Three of the Rawhide *television stars came to Sedalia in 1960 on a promotional tour. They were entertained at lunch at the Bothwell Hotel and posed for pictures—some on horseback—around town. Pictured here, left to right, are: Unidentified, William Hopkins, Eric Fleming of* Rawhide, *and Mayor Abe Silverman. (Sedalia Public Library Collection)*

Above: Eric Fleming and Clint Eastwood pose with some fans at the Missouri Pacific depot. Mr. Fleming drowned a few years later while making a movie in South America. Mr. Eastwood, now sixty-seven, became a major Hollywood star after his Rawhide *days and remains very active in the business as an actor and director. (Ed Brummet Collection)*

Left: Rawhide *stars Clint Eastwood (left) and Eric Fleming practice their fast draws with a young Sedalia fan in the Missouri Pacific depot in 1960. Mr. Eastwood, and probably Mr. Fleming, were made honorary members of the Pettis County Historical Society while in town. (Ed Brummet Collection)*

Above: Sedalia was once known for its trees, especially those on Broadway right of center in this early 1960s aerial view. South Limit has not yet been transformed into Highway 65, but the Jennie Jaynes Lewis Stadium has been built and Heber Hunt School appears to be under construction. (Sedalia Public Library Collection)

Top of page, left: The annual Chamber of Commerce banquets were held in the Smith-Cotton High School cafeteria. Each guest always received a bag full of local products or souvenirs, which this particular year included a loaf of bread. (Sedalia Public Library Collection)

Top of page, right: At the November 5, 1959, annual Chamber of Commerce banquet, Chester Lauck of Continental Oil Company was the speaker. He was formerly "Lum" of Lum and Abner. Pictured left to right are Mr. and Mrs. Del Heckart, Lauck, and William Hopkins. (Sedalia Public Library Collection)

Facing page: Sedalia native son Jack Oakie (born Offield) came home in the fall of 1960 for the city's centennial celebration. The movie comedian is flanked by Miss Sedalia Sandra Hammond on the left and Mrs. Sedalia Helen Eschbacher on the right. (Sedalia Public Library Collection)

SHOES

SEDALIA
F.D.
2

Top of page, left: The building on the northwest corner of Third and Ohio was known as the Ilgenfritz Building for many decades. In the 1950s it was the Gordon Building, and later the Commerce Building. It has survived a fire, an elevator accident, and a notorious attempted arson. In 1960 the building's ground floor was occupied by Penney's, B and B Shoes, and Woolworth's. (Ed Brummet Collection)

Top of page, right: John McGrath organized the Sedalia Bank and Trust Company in 1932 in the old Sedalia Trust Building at Fourth and Ohio. The bank moved to this building (which sported the town's first drive-in window) after World War II. It eventually became part of the Mercantile Bank group and this building was sold to the Open Door Service Center in 1996. (Ed Brummet Collection)

Above: The northwest corner of South Limit and West Sixteenth Street, for years the site of the State Fair Floral Company's greenhouse, was turned into a shopping center in 1965 by W. E. Bingaman. What is now K-Mart had yet to be built. (Sedalia Public Library Collection)

Facing page, above: One of the finest Victorian buildings in Sedalia, the Romanesque-style Kahn Building on the southeast corner of Second and Ohio Streets was doomed by 1960. The tenants were vacating and the city wanted to build parking lots. Today this entire block on the south side of Second Street between Ohio and Lamine is a parking lot. (Ed Brummet Collection)

Facing page, below: The city demolished a row of nineteenth-century buildings in the 100 block of East Main, including what had been the Maple Leaf Club, to build yet another parking lot. (Sedalia Public Library Collection)

Above, left: The 900 block of South Limit (westside) was home to Houchen's Texaco Service, Sherwin-Williams Paints, and the Nu-Way Cafe in 1960. The state would widen Limit a few years later, effectively eliminating parking for these businesses. (Ed Brummet Collection)

Above right: Mules were used to feed cattle on the B. C. Claycomb farm well into the 1950s. Mr. Claycomb (1906–1971) fed hundreds of cattle at a time in five spring-fed feedlots. Fat cattle were shipped to market in Kansas City and St. Louis. (William B. Claycomb Collection)

Above: The Missouri-Kansas Pipe Line Company, soon to be Panhandle Eastern, buried twenty-four miles of pipeline across Pettis County in the early 1930s. This pumping station three miles south of Houstonia at one time employed sixty people, but employs less than half that number now because of automation. (Ed Brummet Collection)

The Boonslick Regional Library bookmobile and staff car makes a visit to Striped College School southeast of Sedalia in the 1960s. The library was organized in 1953 and eventually covered Pettis, Cooper, and Benton Counties with headquarters in Sedalia—although Sedalia was not part of the district. (Sedalia Public Library Collection)

Above: The Katy mainline separates the Smith-Cotton High School tennis courts from the Missouri Public Service power plant. More boys seem to be watching than playing this day. The power plant was demolished in 1992. (Sedalia Public Library Collection)

Above left: The Sedalia Symphony was founded in 1935 and has been performing at the Smith-Cotton auditorium since then. Abe Rosenthal, on the podium, was its conductor for forty-five years. The late Dr. T. S. Hopkins is at the piano on the left. (Sedalia Public Library Collection)

Above, right: The Sedalia Men's Choral Club performed for many years after World War II under the leadership of Abe Rosenthal. Lillian Fox was the pianist. (Sedalia Public Library Collection)

Right: Sedalia has a long tradition of men's concert bands stretching back to the nineteenth century. This is the 1960s version on the new Liberty Park bandstand. Lloyd Knox, center, conducted from 1955 to 1988. (Sedalia Public Library Collection)

Facing page, above: By the 1960s, work at the Missouri Pacific shops had dwindled to a fraction of what it had been fifty years before when they were reported to have been the largest west of the Mississippi River. (Sedalia Public Library Collection)

Above: Bothwell Lodge State Park finally opened to the public in 1979, fifty years after John H. Bothwell's death. Shown here cutting the ribbon, left to right, are: Secretary of State James Kirkpatrick, Representative James Mathewson, an unidentified state official, Senator John Ryan, and an unidentified state official. The park is arguably Pettis County's most scenic spot. (Ed Brummet Collection)

Right: Senator John C. Ryan (1905–1984) pushed the Bothwell Lodge State Park bill through the State Senate at literally the last minute in 1973. Senator Ryan was active in local and state Republican politics for many decades and served three terms as state senator (1966–1970 and 1972–1980). He also worked as a car dealer in Sedalia and owned and operated a 514-acre farm northeast of Sedalia for many years. He is shown here on the far left with his daughter Carolyn Rice and wife Mildred as well as grandchildren James and Cynthia Rice at Bothwell Lodge in May 1979. Longtime Sedalia Democrat *reporter Ron Jennings is in the foreground. (Ed Brummet Collection)*

Senator and Mrs. James L. Mathewson, center, watch as a dignitary signs the guest book on opening day at Bothwell Lodge, May 1979. Senator Mathewson (born 1938) was elected to the Missouri House 1974–1978, then to the Senate 1980–1996, where he served as majority floor leader 1985–1988 and then as President Pro Tem 1989–1996. (Ed Brummet Collection)

Above: In 1920 Houstonia was a thriving town in a productive agricultural area known for its large farms and cattle feeders. It was a stop on the "Lexington Branch" Railroad, supported two banks and a busy downtown. The Depression wiped out the banks, some of the business, and many of the farmers. (Ed Brummet Collection)

Above: The Houstonia Methodist Church was built in 1870 at a cost of $1,700. It escaped the deadly 1875 tornado that destroyed downtown Houstonia. The congregation celebrated its centennial in 1969. (Ed Brummet Collection)

Facing page, above, left: Bothwell Lodge was built in four stages, and had Mr. Bothwell lived a few years longer, his beloved lodge would probably have a somewhat different appearance. A blueprint shows a second tower where the breezeway is and a five-bay balcony across the front instead of this one-bay portico. (William B. Claycomb Collection)

Facing page, above, right: Sedalia businessman and longtime politician Julian Bagby, a staunch Democrat, was a personal friend of President Harry S. Truman, pictured above his head. Mr. Bagby was born and reared on a farm northeast of Green Ridge, and at the time of his death was the largest landowner in Pettis County. His other business interests at one time or another included a chicken hatchery, ice cream plant, and a bottling company. He died in 1988. (Ed Brummet Collection)

Facing page, middle, left: The Hughesville School was built in 1939 and has been extensively enlarged and remodeled since then. The merger of the Hughesville and Houstonia districts in the mid-1960s created Northwest School. (Ed Brummet Collection)

Above: Tyson Foods owns and operates this elevator-feed processing facility at Dresden. The chicken processing plant is a mile east on 1,100 acres. (Ed Brummet Collection)

Top of page: LaMonte's business district surrounds the junction of MO. 127 and U.S. 50. The old business district three-fourths of a mile north is mostly deserted. (Ed Brummet Collection)

Facing page, above & below: In 1910 Dr. R. Seaton Tyler (1855–1940) lost the election for Pettis County representative by one vote out of 7,347 cast. He contested the election, the circuit court found in his favor, and Harvey Dow was forced to vacate his seat in the Missouri House in 1911. Besides his medical practice at Dunksburg, Dr. Tyler owned a 217-acre farm he named "Edgewood." His former home and office are in Dunksburg. (Ed Brummet Collection)

Below, left: Green Ridge's grade school dates from 1870; its high school from 1897. The district became the R-VIII on November 1, 1949. A new building was built in 1962 and there have been several additions since then. (Ed Brummet Collection)

Below, right: Smithton was founded shortly before the Civil War and named in honor of George R. Smith, who was trying to get his own Sedville off the ground seven miles to the west. The Nutrena Feeds elevator is on the right on the site of the old Smithton Creamery. (Ed Brummet Collection)

Below: Green Ridge was founded in 1870–1871 when the Missouri-Kansas and Texas Railway arrived on its way to Fort Scott, Kansas, and the Southwest. The Katy served the town for over a century. Pearl White, silent screen actress, was a native. (Ed Brummet Collection)

Above: The Katy Railroad between St. Charles and Sedalia has become the 200-mile-long Katy Trail State Park. The trail between Beaman, shown here, and Pleasant Green in Cooper County is a scenic section. The trail is expected to be extended to Clinton before the turn of the century. (Ed Brummet Collection)

Left: Beaman was never more than a tiny village with a Katy depot, post office, and Christian Church—all long gone. It was named for Judge J. W. Beeman, a local farmer and county judge, but seems to have always been spelled Beaman. (Ed Brummet Collection)

SITE OF
ST. HELENA
FIRST PETTIS COUNTY SEAT
LOCATED SOUTH AND EAST OF
MUDDY CREEK. ST. HELENA
(ALSO KNOWN AS PIN HOOK)
WAS SETTLED PRIOR TO 1820
AND SERVED AS THE TEMPORARY
PETTIS COUNTY SEAT OF JUSTICE
FROM ORGANIZATION OF THE
COUNTY ON JANUARY 26, 1833,
UNTIL NOVEMBER 6, 1837.
COURT WAS HELD AT RAMEY AND
WASSON'S MILL ONE QUARTER
MILE SOUTHWEST OF THIS POINT.
GEORGETOWN WAS DESIGNATED
THE PERMANENT COUNTY SEAT
IN 1837 AND ST. HELENA WAS
SOON ABANDONED.
ERECTED BY THE PETTIS COUNTY
SESQUICENTENNIAL COMMISSION
1983

Above, left: The SFCC administration building was named in honor of the late William C. Hopkins, longtime president of the board of trustees. (Ed Brummet Collection)

Above, right: The Yeater Building on the campus of State Fair Community College was made possible by a bequest from Mrs. Charles E. Yeater (1880–1972). (Ed Brummet Collection)

Top of page, left: Georgetown served as the Pettis County seat of justice from 1837 to 1865 when George R. Smith persuaded his fellow politicians in Jefferson City to move it to Sedalia. The Georgetown Methodist Church was organized shortly after the Civil War. (Ed Brummet Collection)

Top of page, right: The Georgetown School was the only two-room brick school in the county. It closed in 1968 and is now used by the community for elections and other events. (Ed Brummet Collection)

Facing page: Pettis County observed its sesquicentennial in 1983. In June 1984, the sesquicentennial commission set this stone on Muddy Creek a quarter mile north of the site of St. Helena. Purchased with donations from the public, it was vandalized within the month. (Ed Brummet Collection)

Above: Bothwell Memorial Hospital was Tom Bast's last architectural commission. The original hospital, on the right, was built in 1930. It has been expanded several times since then and is now undergoing another major construction project on the southeast corner. Like most hospitals, each addition reflects the fashion of the day, making for an overall hodgepodge effect. (Ed Brummet Collection)

Top of page: Dr. and Mrs. C. Gordon Stauffacher left $4,000,000 to State Fair Community College to construct this building in 1994. It houses a fine arts gallery (the Goddard Gallery) and classrooms, a theater, and student union/book store. (Ed Brummet Collection)

Facing page, above: The Sedalia Memorial Airport (although no one remembers who or what is memorialized) occupies 392 acres in northeast Sedalia. The current terminal was built in 1979. (Ed Brummet Collection)

Facing page, below: Edward Hurley (1833–1903) was born in Ireland, learned to lay bricks in London, and emigrated to the U.S. in 1854. He arrived in Sedalia in 1872 and in the next thirty years built more of downtown Sedalia than anyone else. He also built his residence, Hurley's Hall, on the southeast corner of West Fifth and Grand. It was converted to four apartments and the wrap-around front porch removed in the early 1960s. Two of the Hurley sons, Tom and Austin, owned Queen City Electric, still operated by Tom's descendants. (Ed Brummet Collection)

Some impressive houses were built on farms, like Rosebriar, built for Mr. and Mrs. Barry Guier in 1993 north of LaMonte. (Ed Brummet Collection)

Below left: This house at 200 West Broadway was built for Mr. and Mrs. John T. Heard in 1904–1906. It has been the home of the Helen G. Steele Music Club and Sorosis for over sixty years. (Ed Brummet Collection)

Below right: Many houses have been constructed in the 1990s in subdivisions west of Sedalia, as was this one, reflecting the general prosperity of the decade. (Ed Brummet Collection)

SEDALIA

Above: Owned by the city, Crown Hill Cemetery dates from Sedalia's earliest years. The Confederates placed their artillery in the cemetery on October 15, 1864, and fired at will into the town's lightly defended fortifications. (William B. Claycomb Collection)

Facing page, above: Once the biggest and busiest (and arguably the ugliest) depot on the Missouri Pacific between Kansas City and St. Louis, the Sedalia depot fell on hard times as the railroad abandoned passenger service in the 1960s. After years of neglect, Downtown Sedalia, Inc. has plans and a grant to restore it and make it once again viable. (Ed Brummet Collection)

Facing page, below, left & right: The Katy Depot, built in 1896, is currently undergoing a $1,000,000 restoration. The Missouri Division of Parks and Historic Preservation is leasing the depot to the Sedalia Chamber of Commerce, which plans to occupy the second floor and sublease the ground floor, which will include a railroad heritage museum. The depot is expected to become a centerpiece of the Katy Trail in the twenty-first century. (Ed Brummet Collection)

Bibliography

Published Sources

Blesh, Rudi. *Scott Joplin: Black-American Classicist,* introduction to *Scott Joplin Collected Piano Works.* New York: The New York Library, 1971.

Cassity, Michael. *Defending a Way of Life: An American Community in the Nineteenth Century.* Albany, New York: State University of New York Press, 1989.

Claycomb, William B. *A History of Northeast Pettis County, Missouri.* Dayton, Ohio: Morningside Press, 1996. (See this book's Selected References for primary sources.)

Devoe, C. Henry. *Sedalia Directory for 1873 and 1874.* Sedalia: Devoe, 1874.

Final Environmental Impact Statement—Deactivation of the Minuteman II Missile Wing at Whiteman Air Force Base, Missouri. Langley, Virginia: 1992.

Harding, Samuel Bannister. *Life of George R. Smith, Founder of Sedalia, Missouri.* Sedalia: n.p., 1904.

Leseur, A. A. *Official Manual of the State of Missouri 1897–98.* Jefferson City: 1898.

McGruder, Mark A. *History of Pettis County, Missouri.* Topeka, Kansas: Historical Publishing Company, 1919.

McVey, W. A. *Yester Years: A Study of Missouri's First Roads and Transportation Systems in Central Missouri.* n.p., 1973.

March, David B. *The History of Missouri.* New York: Lewis Historical Publishing Company, 1967.

North, F. A. *The History of Pettis County, Missouri etc.* n.p., 1882.

Ohman, Marian M. *Encyclopedia of Missouri Courthouses.* Columbia, Missouri: University of Missouri—Columbia, Extension Division, 1981.

Polk's Sedalia City Directory, Including Pettis County. Kansas City: R. L. Polk & Company, 1958.

Silver Anniversary State Fair Community College 1968–1993. Sedalia: 1993.

United States Census Reports for Pettis County, Missouri. 1840–1880.

Bibliography

Manuscripts

Claycomb, William B. *The Rise and Decline of a Midwest Railroad Hub: Sedalia, Missouri*, 1997.

Claycomb, William B. *Whiskey by Prescription: A Local Profile*, 1996.

Judge Henry Lamm Reflects on the Old Pettis County Courthouse, Sedalia: The Pettis County Historical Society newsletter, May 13, 1983.

McVey, W. A. *The Sounds of Early Sedalia*, 1984.

Maps and Atlases

Map of Pettis County, Missouri. Philadelphia: Warner & Foote, 1876.

Plat Book of Pettis County, Missouri. Philadelphia: North West Publishing Company, 1896.

Plat Book of Pettis County, Missouri. Philadelphia: A. R. Stinson, 1916.

Newspapers

Houstonia (Missouri) Leader, Special Good Roads Magazine, October 5, 1928.

Sedalia Daily Capital, April 28, 1896, passim.

Sedalia Democrat, August 3, 1979, passim.

Index

Index

Index

Index

About the Author

William B. Claycomb, born in Sedalia, Missouri, and reared on a farm east of Hughesville, is a graduate of Hughesville High School and the University of Missouri–Columbia (1966). After two years' service in the U.S. Army during the Vietnam War, he spent twenty years engaged in banking, real estate, and bank regulation activities. He retired in 1989 as the first state training coordinator for the Missouri Division of Finance in Jefferson City, and has since devoted his time to research and writing.

Mr. Claycomb has published numerous scholarly articles about Pettis Countians, and in 1996 published *A History of Northeast Pettis County, Missouri* (reprint 1997). He resides on his family's farm, purchased by his great-grandfather in 1869.

About the Photograph Editor

Edward Eugene Brummet was born and has lived most of his life in Sedalia. He is a graduate of Smith Cotton High School. He then became employed at the *Sedalia Democrat and Capital* for twenty years. Upon retiring from the newspaper, he became a prominent photographer and is still in business in Sedalia.

251